G000241557

The Hazelnut Grove

Paula Read

LEAF BY LEAF

Published by Leaf by Leaf
an imprint of Cinnamon Press
Meirion House, Tanygrisiau, Blaenau Ffestiniog, Gwynedd, LL41 3SU
www.cinnamonpress.com
The right of Paula Read to be identified as author of this work has been
asserted by her in accordance with the Copyright, Designs and Patent Act,
1988. Copyright © 2020 JPaula Read
ISBN: 978-1-78864-914-8
British Library Cataloguing in Publication Data. A CIP record for this
book can be obtained from the British Library.
*All rights reserved. No part of this publication may be reproduced, stored in a retrieval
system, or transmitted in any form or by any means, electronic, mechanical, photocopying,
recording or otherwise without the prior written permission of the publishers. This book
may not be lent, hired out, resold or otherwise disposed of by way of trade in any form
of binding or cover other than that in which it is published, without the prior consent of
the publishers.*
Designed and typeset in Garamond by Cinnamon Press.
Cover design by Adam Craig © Adam Craig.
Cinnamon Press is represented in the UK by Inpress Ltd and in Wales by
the Books Council of Wales.

Acknowledgements

Huge thanks to my cousin and his wife for inviting me into their
lives and, of course, for making my research so very enjoyable. If I
behaved intrusively, they never treated me with anything but
courtesy and kindness. And thank you to my aunt who is the most
entertaining of companions.

I also owe a great debt to my creative writing teachers at City,
University of London, for their excellent guidance, and to my
fellow students, whose critical judgement was always so useful.

Thank you to my editors at Cinnamon Press, for making this
possible.

Homage to the memory of my mother and father for the gift of
love.

And to my dear family, who patiently read and re-read the text, I
owe everything. Thank you Hans, most thorough and incisive of
editors, and Lily, who writes the best, most encouraging and
generous notes, and Roland, master of technical matters and the
laconic comment.

The Hazelnut Grove

For *la maison française*
where we are happiest

PREFACE

Sarah is combing Allegra in the courtyard. She is trying to untangle the fringe obscuring Allegra's bright brown eyes, but the small dog is making it difficult, tossing her head from Sarah who pursues her with even more determination. They enjoy themselves.

I am sitting with Daisy, my aunt, at the stone mosaic table overlooking the garden, watching Sarah as she squats on her haunches to attend to the dog, her short blond hair tucked behind her ears. She is a slightly built woman in her early fifties and looks nowhere near her age—nor does Luke, her husband and my younger cousin, lean as a greyhound and almost as laid-back. Daisy is Luke's mother, my late mother's younger sister, a slim woman (she swims three times a week) and just eighty (much to her disgust, but then as the family always says, it's better than the alternative). She adds dash to any outfit, even the creased linen shorts and white shirt she is wearing now.

It is early summer. Around Sarah and Allegra, several large earthenware pots are arranged in symmetry. Olive and fig trees grow in them, while in smaller pots, herbs are thriving. The basil is particularly vivid, bright green and each leaf perfect, not one bite mark left by some marauding predator. The house itself, *Cascina Cannella*, literally 'Cinnamon Farmhouse,' is named in memory of their last English cat, a charmingly plump tabby whose plumpness extended to the pads of his paws.

Sarah sets Allegra free and comes to the stone table to join us. There are still a couple of slices of breakfast cake in the bread basket, light sponge with apricots baked into the top, picked from the garden and nicely embedded in the cake.

Do we want more coffee? No, cake morsels are sufficient. We sit looking out over the small copse of fruit trees, a couple of hammocks slung between them. Rosemary, thyme and lavender scramble out from the rocks leading down to the trees. And then, over there, lies the top of the vineyard that stretches away down the hillside. In the autumn, they harvest the Moscato grapes and send them to the nearest winemaker in Asti. The wine from their vineyard is sweet and golden, a perfect pudding wine.

On a previous visit, over several evenings of chat and Dolcetto, a local red wine, we all decided it would be a great idea to tell Sarah and Luke's story and that I should be the one to do it, given my background in journalism. All of us in the family are aware of how Sarah and Luke bought a dilapidated old farmhouse in rural Piedmont and subsequently made the momentous decision almost fifteen years ago to move to Italy permanently. The three sisters, my late mother Violet, her older sister May, and Daisy, were remarkably close, which meant they maintained a family cohesion. All the cousins knew what was going on in each other's lives. The idea, however, of telling Sarah and Luke's story to a wider audience than the immediate family developed slowly, like all the best wines. Piedmont is, after all, one of the most renowned wine-growing regions in Italy. It is the place where you find the great Barolos and Barbarescos, although my favourite is the light and tasty Dolcetto. Wine flows through this story, a happy emollient, in contrast to the scratchy underside of the tale, in which loneliness and fear play their part. It is a story of determination, obstinacy and joy—and of the unexpected.

Luke and Sarah are not their real names. We have decided to change the names of the characters in the book to protect their privacy. Not everything has been a walk in the sunshine in this mountain retreat. Much has happened that might have driven them away, especially Sarah who is not tied to an Italian heritage like Luke. His father, Gino Rinaldi, was born in England of Italian parents.

Their story seems almost as significant to me as my own, which in a sense, it is. A few years before Sarah and Luke looked for a house in Italy, my family had already bought what might loosely be termed a habitable house in rural France (it had running water, a working electric supply and a bidet but no toilet). It was 1992. This wasn't so unusual. Many people in Britain were encouraged to widen their horizons and think about spending the money that might have been earmarked for holidays abroad for a more ambitious purpose—putting it towards buying their own property in Europe. Borders could be crossed easily. People were curious. There was a willingness to embrace the differences between us. Europe signified space and adventure and shared history, something to be part of, not as it does now in these distorted times, a place to escape from.

*

On Saturday 23 June 2018 I took part in a protest march in London calling for a people's vote on the final deal agreed by the UK government on the country's withdrawal from the European Union, or Brexit. This was an anti-Brexit march, with participants drawn from all over the UK, all intent on demonstrating how much we wanted to stay in the EU and how frightened we were of leaving it. For many of us, this march was unbelievable. Unbelievable because we were still suffering from the shock of the vote to leave the EU on 23 June 2016. How could 'the British people' make such a suicidal decision? The vote was close, but the outcome held up as decisive, despite the many doubts about the organisation of the referendum or the number of people voting only representing a portion of the population. Not everyone was allowed a vote. Many British citizens living abroad in Europe, for example, could not vote, even though they were bound to be affected by the outcome.

Leaving the EU is a catastrophe for many and a step away from the vision of a safer Europe many have striven for after the world wars of the twentieth century. That vision was of a progressive union, built on the determination to avoid pitching ourselves back into that pit of political helplessness that engendered hatred and genocide. We hoped for the creation of great and democratic institutions where talking and compromise could take place, where pragmatism and fairness would win and dangerous ideologies would find no takers.

That vision was deluged in hateful rhetoric, the expression of ugly attitudes and the legitimation of lies. And here we are now, exposing our children and grandchildren to a future of division, more hatred, more lies.

When I started writing this book, the most significant decision for a generation in Britain had not yet been taken. This is a book about following a dream, one shared by many, but one that only a few manage to fulfil—the dream of making your life in another country of your choice, choosing how you live rather than accepting the place and culture you are born into. It was possible to make such a dream come true then because of another equally significant decision made by the British people in 1973.

In that year, the UK voted to join the EU, seeking not only a better economic future but a more secure one. That decision opened not only the physical borders to many other countries and cultures, it also opened the eyes, the minds and the hearts of British citizens many of whom travelled to Europe for the first time.

*

There is always a wind in the evening. In the summer, it is welcome, lifting heat from shoulders. You are sitting on the balcony furthest from the main house, looking across and around the valley. Below and over to the side, you can discern through the balcony railing the top branches of the trees in the shadowy hazelnut grove. Lights are distributed sparingly across the broad, dark slopes. People and animals are settling into the warm night.

The farm dogs have nothing to bark at. The occasional light moving in a series of S bends shows people are still on the move, negotiating the sinuous mountain roads. On a summer's evening it's easy to feel that there is no more beautiful place on earth.

But turn to the winter. Then there is no sitting on the balcony furthest from the main house. It's too cold. The wind is bitter and sometimes the snow is in vast piles, weighing down the trees in the hazelnut grove that stands to the side of the house and around which curves the road.

Then, *Cascina Cannella* could be considered almost as some mediaeval fortification, some mountaintop fastness only reached by the steadfast and determined.

The building of life in *Cascina Cannella* is a fairy tale, but one in which the characters have had to draw on amounts of courage and self-reliance they might never have discovered in themselves if they had chosen a different life. *The Hazelnut Grove* is a story of moving to another country in search of a dream, but one that recognises what such an adventure demands. What if you sell all your worldly goods, abandon a home you have been building for years in the country of your birth, quit a job you enjoy, say goodbye to your family and friends, and give up entirely that certain place of safety, to take a chance on a dream that at times becomes an ordeal? This is what happened to Luke and Sarah.

11

They remain, still, blithely indifferent to the political machinations of either the country of their birth or the country that is their home. The politics of governments do not seem to reach them here on their hillside. They can gaze out over a timeless landscape and feel safe in their enchanted world. Will this last?

The late Italian writer Natalia Ginzburg wrote in 1951, a few years after the end of the Second World War, of how intimately connected we are and yet how we fail to communicate with one another. She had reason to be disquieted. Her husband Leone Ginzburg died in the prison of Regina Coeli in Rome after beatings and torture by the German police. The German forces were occupying the northern half of Italy, after the fall of Italy's fascist leader Benito Mussolini in 1943.

It seems that, in many European countries, the old post-Second World War certainties are crumbling. Trust in the great democratic institutions diminishes, fears about immigration rise and metastasize, truth is a distortion so that free speech becomes speech without responsibility. There is a swelling of ignorance and even pride in that ignorance. The expectation that things will continue as they are, that you can live your life undisturbed, may no longer be based on sound foundations, if it ever was.

Sarah and Luke are residents in an adopted land, voluntary exiles. They feel at home, but are they safe?

CHAPTER 1
The House on the Hill

Piedmont, Italy
May 1999

It was as if the occupants had just stepped out to run an errand or two and not returned. Inside the house, it was cooler, dark and smelled of mushrooms, mouse urine and cold stone... there was still a smell of smoke from a leaking chimney. Personal belongings were scattered. In the kitchen, a plastic water bottle hung from a hook by the small, stained sink, its porcelain surface crazed with a spider's web of thin cracks. And by the sink lay a piece of dried soap, blackened and streaky, next to a limp towel. Family photographs with curling edges lay on surfaces. Old copies of *Famiglia Cristiana* (*Christian Family*) were piled in corners. There was an old sewing machine in a large wooden cupboard and a very small television perched on a tall narrow table.

They breathed damp, musty air. The soil floors were green with mould in places. Hazelnut shells were everywhere, discarded by the only occupants, the mice and rats.

Sarah knew it was the house for them...

*

The house did not seduce them at first. As they approached it via a dirt track, Sarah and Luke's initial impressions were that the building was nothing special. As they turned the corner to its front, the house was obscured by vast spreading fig trees and fierce undergrowth. Together, they formed a huge, three-metre-high hedge. It might have been the setting for 'Sleeping Beauty', so tall and forbidding were the trees, so abundant the growth.

An apricot tree and two fig trees stood guard as Luke and Sarah fought their way through the vegetation to reach the house, which was there, waiting for them.

Shutters hung off their hinges; all the protective metal bars on the kitchen windows were bent, probably by thieves, according to their estate agent *Signora* Gallo.

They walked around the stone house, which was large, simply constructed and clad in a decaying buttermilk plaster. At the back and standing at a right angle to it was the hayloft. It was full of old wicker wine baskets and planks of wood and makeshift rabbit hutches.

Inside, downstairs, there were two large rooms on either side of the staircase. Upstairs, there were two large front bedrooms and an empty derelict space at the back, where a crude bathroom had been constructed. At least, this was what the house literature said. In reality, it was like a kind of pokey downstairs toilet that you might find in an English house, but located upstairs.

The plumbing was primitive—in fact, pretty much non-existent. The toilet waste simply flowed down a delightful orange plastic tube that descended to the cellar and then opened out onto the neighbour's land.

The ceilings of each room were vaulted. Sarah could see that beneath the flaking paint and plaster, there would be brick vaults and wooden beams. She could almost picture how they would be if she could get her hands on them. The house was furnished but had been left empty for some eight years. You would not have guessed, though. Sarah had the sensation the owners might return at any time to collect their scattered belongings.

The surrounding air was warm from the May sunshine. Derelict though it was, the house seemed to welcome them; its smells and decay did not have the tang of the cold and the dank. Instead, it offered the lightly toasted flavours of musty rooms, long unused, and of other people's possessions, their faint perfume released in the awakening softness of the air. The approaching summer held the promise of luxurious heat and light, which they craved after working through another overcast and rainy English winter.

Then they entered the main bedroom and pushed open the old wooden shutters. What they saw took their breath away—a timeless Italian mountainside stretching before them, covered in miniature vineyards, all bearing Moscato grapes. The vines were distributed in neat rows down the hillside. Blossoming fruit and nut trees were all around—apricot, Morello cherry, hazelnut—so much space, so much sky. Across the valley, Luke and Sarah gazed upon other vine-clad hillsides.

That day in May 1999 was warm and pleasant. There was a light breeze. This was it.

*

Summer always meant Italy. It was where Luke and Sarah came for their holidays, leaving England behind with its lowering skies and everyday pressures. And it was where they were happiest, whatever the region.

They used to fly to Italy, renting a car there to explore the different regions—roaming through Tuscany, Abruzzo, Apulia, Calabria—on and on, never able to decide on a favourite, each place exerting its own powerful attractions. This was the 1990s, at least two decades before the 2016 British referendum on leaving Europe, when belonging to the European Union seemed incontrovertible. European borders were open. People in Britain were unconstrained by fear of the unknown, of being unable to speak the language, of Europeans doing things differently. They were free to explore, learn and experience the unfamiliar. They were used to this freedom. They had grown up with it.

Despite the limitations of travelling on an aircraft, Luke and Sarah managed to return to England laden with bottles of wine, always Italian of course. They tested the limit as to how many bottles you can physically bring back, squashed into a suitcase, on a regular flight—apparently, thirty-eight.

The miracle of the channel tunnel, which opened in 1994, meant they could travel directly to the continent by car, avoiding the fuss of airports or bouncing across the ocean on the ferry, save time and money on car rentals and, importantly, stay in control of their own itinerary and destinations. This was much too great an opportunity to pass up. Luke was almost incapable of controlling the quantity of bottles of wine he felt compelled to buy. It was too easy to say, 'Oh just one more, we can fit it in.' But of course, one bottle then became an entire case.

On one occasion, there was just no room in the car for the wine. Even after packing the car with dirty washing to act as padding in every nook and cranny to optimise the amount of usable space, the problem was still unresolved. There were just too many bottles.

Eyes narrowed in silent concentration, Luke contemplated his wife, a small slender woman who didn't take up much space, then contemplated the remainder of the wine that they had not managed to fit into the car. Ultimately, he came down in favour of Sarah's company rather than using her spot to pack the rest of the wine, but it was close…

At one point, Luke had around 1,000 bottles stored in England, but was nevertheless single-minded in his pursuit of another wine to try, another wine to introduce to his willing tasters among family and friends. All of this was an indication that what began as one of Luke's principal passions, would one day become a way of maintaining an independent life, working for himself as a freelance supplier of Italian wine to his discerning circle of friends. On those Italian holidays, Sarah was no slouch in stocking the car with Italian food either. Heavenly journeys, although at the time she was stuffed in like an inferior box of vegetables, the cases of wine taking up the most comfortable positions. But still, heavenly—the air in the car suffused with all those smells of the produce grown in earth warmed by an Italian sun.

So when the small ad appeared in the back of *Decanter* magazine on that day in April 1998, it could not have presented itself to more susceptible readers.

With no serious thoughts about buying a vineyard, or looking at Italian property, Luke nevertheless sent for more information. Seven days later, a large, brown envelope arrived. The company appeared professional and had included literature on the local area, a guide to buying houses in Italy, as well as information on the actual houses. Most were expensive, but three did not seem unreasonable. Luke and Sarah, with no intention of buying a house in Italy, studied them closely.

*

Think back to the late 1990s. The internet was not yet all pervasive. Sarah and Luke had made plans to go on holiday in May of 1999 to northern Tuscany. A detour of some three hours to Piedmont in Italy's northwest was not such a big deal. A three-hour drive to see three houses. Still daydreaming, off they went. After all, they had no intention of buying a house, it was just one of those things you sometimes do on holiday (or this was what Sarah believed for the longest time; for Luke living in Italy was one of his life's ambitions, but one he kept relatively quiet. He didn't want to scare Sarah away from the idea). They did not do any research on what other house agencies might be around in Italy at the time—no internet, so it would not have been easy. They did not choose the area.

'The house chose us.'

They had arranged to meet the estate agent in a bar in a small town with several café/bars, a hardware shop, some food and general stores and restaurant or two, all surrounding a sandy market square, fringed on all four sides with hazel trees. Luke and Sarah were curious about what they would find. Would estate agents in Italy be honest in their descriptions of the properties? What did 'habitable' mean? Habitable for humans or mice? Running water? Would that be from a tap or down the walls?

The day arrived. It was after 11am and a pleasant 22 degrees Celsius. Sarah and Luke sat in the designated bar, drinking espresso. Cappuccino would have been out of order. No Italian would order it that late in the morning. Above all, they wanted to fit in, not stand out as English tourists. Sarah was surprised to find that she felt nervous and also oddly self-conscious. She looked down at her dress. It was a light blueish cotton and quite short. Too short? There was quite a lot of slender thigh sticking out from under the dress. She crossed her legs, tugged at her dress a bit, then took out a mirror from the small rucksack she had set down against the metal chair leg. She grimaced, ran her fingers through the short bob of blond hair.

Luke glanced at her, smiling.

'You look great. Really tanned.'

'Are you nervous?'

'Well, I suppose so. Yes, a bit.'

'You can do all the talking—I can't even think of a single word in Italian at the moment.' Sarah scowled in a mock self-deprecatory way.

'Is that her?'

A small woman with reddish hair, pulled straight back into a tight chignon, was approaching. Was she the agent? She was looking around as if searching for someone. She looked straight through them, so Luke took the initiative, 'Are you *Signora* Gallo?' he asked in his imperfect Italian.

The woman was rather taken aback.

'Yes,' she replied, as she scrutinised them closely.

Luke and Sarah had thought they looked smart. Luke was dressed in shirt and trousers, rather than his usual loose t-shirt and shorts. Sarah's dress was a nod towards the potential formality of the meeting. She preferred a t-shirt and shorts too.

It was obvious *Signora* Gallo was suspicious of them. Were they time wasters? In fact, later in the day, it became clear that this was what she had thought at first—that they were students with no intention of buying. At that point, Sarah and Luke were already thirty-five years old and Luke's fine blond hair was starting to show signs of grey.

Still, they were not what *Signora* Gallo was expecting. The area of Piedmont was becoming a target area for foreigners seeking second homes, particularly the well-off northern Europeans.

Signora Gallo had arranged for them to see the three houses during the day, which didn't seem a huge number, but the many winding roads and hills meant it would take nearly the whole day to see them all, even though they were all local.

Ghosts

The first house was situated up a dirt track next to some non-Italian inhabitants with a very noisy, menacing dog. Not a good start.

Sarah was spooked from the outset, her skin tingled with goose bumps. It felt like the original owners were still here, as if they were planning to share the house with the new inhabitants. This would have been difficult, of course, as they were dead.

Luke was not going to be put off. There is a steeliness inside the amiable persona he presents to the world. The two of them continued to wander around the house.

It was also filthy, which wasn't going to endear it to Sarah. The rooms were covered in a slick of dirt, not simply the dust of time, but the ingrained dirt of things never having been cleaned thoroughly. Food was strewn around and there was mould in the kitchen sink.

Luke and Sarah both felt disappointed. But what had they expected? And anyway, they kept telling themselves, it's not like we're definitely going to do this. One thing this first visit did was lower their expectations drastically.

*

Signora Gallo drove them to the second house. As the road wound up a steep hill, Luke and Sarah kept expecting to come on the house at every turn. They were growing more and more tense. When these two get tense, rather than quarrel, they become very, very quiet. They had virtually stopped breathing as they neared the top of the hill, so fiercely were they holding their breath. And then, just when they figured they would never reach the top, there it was. Their house, perched above its vineyard, looking out over the hills, all of them covered in vineyards.

And, there and then, it felt as if they had driven home.

CHAPTER 1 *bis (Chapter 1a)*

When my husband and I set off back in 1992 to look for a house in France that a) we could afford and b) had a roof and walls, just like Sarah and Luke, we were also ridiculously disappointed at what we were first shown. We had been seduced into thinking that abandoned picturesque houses in rural areas were ripe to be purchased by keen but not rich outsiders. We left the two children, just two and four years old, with my parents, who were willing babysitters, in a highly unsuitable cottage with a slippery spiral staircase and everything within reach of inquisitive fingers. And we left the two dogs in familiar kennels, but still howling, as we drove off to the ferry port to spend five days exploring the bargains of Normandy.

One of the first houses we were shown by our estate agent *Monsieur* Duval, a suave, portly gentleman with an immaculately pointed beard, looked like an air raid shelter. It was situated by the side of a country road, built from some mix of breeze block and stone, and rendered in a grey glaze of concrete. Inside, it was painted a mournful green. I felt like I was in an empty swimming pool with mould on the walls. It was a nightmare. Really? This was what was on offer for our budget? Let's just pack and go home. We were depressed.

But then *Monsieur* D mentioned the Normandy beaches. We perked up. Could we afford a house near the beach? Indeed we could. The second house we were shown was not so much near the beach, as an integral part of the beach. The sand had backed up onto the rear wall of the house so that when you went in via the front door, you were overwhelmed by the darkness. Where you might have expected light, there was only shade. All the windows at the back of the house were blocked with sand piles. It was as if a sand storm in some Arabian desert had swept through and half buried the building. This was a house you would have to excavate before you could enter it.

I was familiar, therefore, with that sinking feeling when it becomes clear that what you might have fantasised about, almost despite yourself, may be unavailable.

And yet, miraculously, our house found us, just as their hidden house found Sarah and Luke. I will never forget the moment in November 1992 when we drove up the narrow farm lane and saw the French house, our house, alone on a patch of wildly grassy land, its honey-grey stone walls bathed in the mist of a Norman morning.

CHAPTER 2
A vineyard of our own

The house hidden behind the trees had stolen their hearts. Luke and Sarah could think of nothing for the rest of the holiday. Back in England, they made the decision to buy it. Only one viewing, no survey. Were they mad? Chasing a dream? Yes and yes. But, as Sarah says, 'it felt right.'

It wasn't a secret to anyone who knew Luke Rinaldi that his dream was to live in Italy. One of the reasons is evident in his name. He grew up with a father, Gino Rinaldi, who was born in England but whose roots were Italian and who looked Italian and who behaved like a lot of English people's idea of an Italian. He was a small man with a quiff of dark hair, expressive hands and an eye for women. He spoke English as if it ought to be Italian. He was not what you usually found in a Lancashire seaside town in the mid twentieth century.

Gino didn't grow up in northern England. Luke never knew his paternal grandmother, the Italian woman who died giving birth to the three-pound (1.36 kg) baby Gino— and to a twin sister, who weighed five pounds (2.27 kg) but who did not survive. Luke's mother Daisy (my aunt) recounts how the family transported the surviving boy from the north to the south of England to be brought up by his paternal aunt who had married an Englishman and who now lived in the south (*'they took him on a train, all the while rubbing him in cod liver oil.'*). This was where the handsome young Gino was raised and where he eventually met and married the exceptionally pretty Daisy, with her short curly hair and 'the best pair of legs in the county.' They were each barely twenty years old.

Their honeymoon was in Tuscany, the birthplace of Gino's dead mother, before Tuscany became dismissive shorthand for the champagne socialists of the English middle classes, or admiring shorthand for the beauty of Italy, depending on your taste. This was the 1960s. Daisy had never been abroad before *('people didn't did they?')*, nor had she drunk wine. On their honeymoon, they drank Orvieto, a pale yellow wine tasting of citrus fruits and apples, which Daisy never drinks these days without mentioning the honeymoon connection.

Gino then plucked Daisy from her southern roots and they moved from south to north to join the wider family's business. The north seemed to Daisy's family an immense distance. It might as well have been Tuscany in their eyes.

Daisy always maintained an ambivalent relationship with the Italian side of the family. She remembers stepping out of line a couple of times (she never learned not to), expressing views the family found unacceptable. 'Don't ever, *ever* go against the family,' she was warned, a fist in her face or a pointed finger at her nose, depending on the accuser.

Nevertheless, Daisy couldn't help but be entranced by aspects of Gino's background. It was so eventful and exotic, compared with her sedate upbringing in the dour post-war years in southern England. Luke's childhood was steeped in things Italian because of Gino. This Italian connection, the apparent romance of Italy, seen from a great distance and experienced only through holidays and the softened and somewhat rose-tinted views of Italian relatives long settled in England, suffused the lives of Luke and his older brother and sister. Their father's story, with its grief-stricken beginning, coloured their lives. Italian-American crooners Tony Bennett and Frank Sinatra provided the soundtrack they heard around the house as they were growing up. The family all agreed that Gino looked like Tony Bennett, with his distinctive nose and wolfish smile. Italy represented a beautiful ideal, something different from the everyday, a place of dreams.

Luke was particularly susceptible to the dream. He was drawn to the history of the land of his father's ancestors and tells the stories told to him of the partisans trudging through mountains, their broken feet clad only in cardboard. He felt most keenly the prejudice his father suffered as a man of Italian ancestry living in post-Second World War Britain ('*you fucking wop*' was a common epithet). For most of his adult life he had fantasised about living in Italy, preparing for such a possibility from an early age, choosing to learn Italian at school, for example, not something your average fifteen-year-old boy in England does.

His was a disrupted life at that point. His parents were divorcing (that eye for the women) and decided to send him, the baby of the family, to boarding school in an effort to protect him from the fallout. He lived in the school during the week, apart from the rest of the family, only coming home on weekends. Maybe the fact that, in effect, he left home earlier than he might have expected gave him the courage to pursue the Italian dream more doggedly.

He made at least three attempts to achieve this, even before he met Sarah.

In one of these attempts, Luke had been lured to Sicily, ostensibly to learn the wine trade. He was working for a pet food producing company, just twenty-three years old, and dreaming more about wine than dog biscuits.

'I left my job after one and a half years because I got an offer from a guy when I went on a trip to Sicily, to come and run a wine business for him in northeast Italy, I thought it was my big chance. Turned out I was wrong...'

'What came of that?' I ask.

'Nothing. What came of that was experience of life.' Luke returned to the UK after just four weeks.

So what went wrong?

'It was January, it was freezing cold, it was snowing and when I got there, I was expecting him to take me to a completed winery, where I would be learning about the wine, learning about the business.' Luke could see it all—he would become the manager, eventually, be responsible for the winery and at such a young age too.

But when they arrived at the… winery, it turned out to be a ruin. Work was supposed to be starting on it that week. The Sicilian expected Luke to get stuck in and do everything he said. He wasn't significantly older than Luke, but he ordered him around as if he were a particularly aggressive paterfamilias.

'That meant getting the witch's broom and cleaning all the cobwebs off the roof—I don't know why I was doing that, because the building all had to come down anyway.'

Three things stick in Luke's mind from that time. He and the Sicilian were both staying in the same hotel. Luke's Italian was still quite basic. They communicated tortuously —Luke struggling to understand, the Sicilian making no allowances for his limited language, speaking always at a rapid-fire pace. He asked Luke if they made wine in England. The perfect question because Luke's leaving present when he quit his job at the food company was the World Atlas of Wine.

'I'd been reading it because I thought it might be useful for what I was about to do.' Luke has a rueful expression. 'Winemaking in England was just starting in those days. So I said there's very little, but yes there are vineyards in England, they're making sparkling wines in the south of England and Kent. And he replied: "No they're not." I said: "Yes they are." He said: "No they're not. You can't believe everything you read in books." I thought, hang on, I've just come out of university, I thought that was what life was all about.'

The second thing Luke remembers is thinking ahead and wondering if he could get down to Sicily, to the winery there that was already up and running.

'Why don't I go and learn things in Sicily?' he asked the Sicilian.

'You've got things to learn here.'

So that didn't work.

And the third thing is the car episode. The Sicilian had a Citroen 2CV 'a bit like Mum's.' We grin, thinking of Daisy's beloved yellow Citroen with the brown stripe

'It was freezing cold—because it does get very cold in the northeast—and his car wouldn't start. He got out, looked under the bonnet, couldn't do anything about it, so he shouted at me: "Come and watch me, watch me and learn how to do it, don't just sit there, watch me and learn what to do."'

Luke is imitating the Godfather here.

'I thought that's it, *finito*. So over dinner one night, I told him. I said, "I'm sorry, I'm not going through with this, I've decided to go back home." He blanked me, the whole time. From that moment on, he never said another word to me.

'When he took me to the station to get the train, I thought: he hasn't given me my money yet, he hasn't given me any money; I need that money to get home. I asked him for it: "Can I have my money please." So he got out his money, started counting it and then just threw it at me. And that was it, *ciao, ciao.*'

The Sicilian had transformed from paterfamilias to sulky teenager. This did not deter Luke from his pursuit of the Italian dream. Of course it didn't. Luke had grown up believing in the dream of Italy; he had been nourished on stories of the courage and resilience of Italians. He had spent childhood holidays in one or other sun-dappled Italian village. He could not forget the scents of the rosemary, the thyme, the oregano growing in the hot yellow earth. The Sicilian drama just made him more determined. It did not define, nor contain, Luke's version of Italy

*

In many ways, it is easy to understand how Luke came to the conclusion that Italy could become his permanent home. How, then, did Sarah get drawn into this romance? For Sarah, the move was a much greater leap into the dark. She had a lot more to lose. And as it turned out, she had a lot more to endure.

For Sarah, there was much to fear.

She grew up in the UK's black country, the youngest of four children. She hasn't a drop of Italian blood. In fact, she seems almost the opposite of the standard Italian stereotype in many British imaginations of the vivacious extrovert, with the energetic hand gestures and apparent willingness to display emotion. (Observers of Italian society argue against the veracity of such stereotypes. A foreigner arriving in Italy might think everyone goes around saying '*Ciao*' to each other in a relaxed and carefree way, but they don't. '*Ciao*' means 'Hi' and an Italian would not greet someone they don't know well in this way. Just as in every society, Italians live by unspoken rules.)

'I'm quite timid,' Sarah says, 'I was quite a timid person as a child. I fought to get over this timidity.'

Luke doesn't fit this stereotype either, but has been born with a certain deftness of character that allows him to welcome you into his world, but always on his terms, very much the negotiator. He and Sarah met at university in England's Midlands when they were both eighteen. Both studied food science and nutrition. And both found jobs in the food supply industry. So far, so normal. They had been together for over a decade before the notion of a home in Italy—ostensibly a holiday home—seriously crept into their thinking.

Sarah and Luke loved their English life. It was good, containing all the things people think they want. They bought a house in southern England. They enjoyed doing it up. Sarah particularly loved the garden—all herbaceous perennials, herbs and cottage garden charmers. All their cats, and there have been quite a few, are named after herbs and spices—English cats have English herb and spice names, but Italian cats are a cut above and have Italian herb and spice names. From Cinnamon to *Origan* (Oregano), the cats are their constant companions.

Adding an Italian holiday to this life was going to be an awfully big adventure.

The plan evolved out of the conjunction of a variety of circumstances. Or it was written in the stars. Or written in a wine magazine.

Luke regularly bought the wine magazine, *Decanter*, particularly if there was anything in it about Italian wine. Even in those days, Luke was passionate about Italian wine, comparing it favourably with French wine while dismissing any claims New World wines might make. He collected and stored it in the most unusual places in the house. Luke also had an overflow of bottles in his friend's cellar. Wine, like the cats, was a constant in Luke and Sarah's lives and in the lives of their friends and families.

On the day they spotted the small advert for Italian vineyards for sale at the back of the magazine, they each—separately—imagined themselves living in Italy, with a vineyard even. An Italian vineyard to themselves. They didn't immediately confide these flights of fancy to each other. It seemed too far-fetched—at first.

Not that they were planning to move to Italy. It would be fun to look at houses, check out the possibility of buying a holiday home. Would a house they could afford be a house they could live in? Would it just be some dilapidated ruin? How much work would they have to do? Did they really want to commit to going to the same place every holiday? Were they just kidding themselves? After all, wasn't it one of those daydreams people hardly ever act on?

CHAPTER 2 *bis*

When we saw our house in France initially, it was still being lived in. We signed the purchase papers at the notary's office in the presence of the owners, a well-fed French couple from Paris, comfortably past middle age and ready to move somewhere else in France with more settled weather. The Cotentin peninsula is a paradise for weather enthusiasts. Clouds can scud so fast across the sky the eye can barely follow their movement. Sunshine can blaze for warm, lovely moments and then is banished by clouds like battleships that hove into the path of the sun's rays. When the wind dies and the air is still, you look behind you nervously. Where can the wind be lurking?

We were on good terms with *Monsieur* and *Madame* and spent the evening together in the local restaurant, famous for its *tripes de Caen* (tripe cooked in the Caen fashion). Tripe refers to the lining of an animal's stomach, most often the first three stomachs of a cow. Caen is the capital of the *Basse Normandie* region, sacrificed like much of Normandy to the aims of the Allied forces in the Second World War, and bombed to smithereens during the 1944 Battle of Normandy. I think we ate the tripe, so happy were we to be allowed our patch of France.

The house had just two large rooms when we bought it, along with a half-renovated attic above the bedroom that could only be reached by climbing a ladder propped against the outside wall and wriggling in through the narrow window, set almost at floor level in the attic. In the larger of the two rooms, the kitchen/living room, the family had left behind two cooking stoves that took up the space in the monumental stone fireplace and an (almost) lethal paraffin stove for heating. When we first saw the house, it also contained many, many beds. It seemed as if the family had used it as a place to sleep and eat. The couple had sons who spent their holidays enthusiastically mussel-collecting, fishing and hunting land-based creatures for food. We imagined the great greasy feasts of meat and fish they must have consumed before collapsing onto the beds arranged around the walls of the kitchen, facing in pragmatic fashion the food-producing area.

CHAPTER 3
The Eyes of the Madonna

The purchase

They bought the house. They named it *Cascina Cannella* (Cinnamon Farmhouse) after their cat. The year was 1999.

In those first months of getting used to becoming the owners of their piece of Italy, in an unfamiliar landscape and a culture they only knew at a superficial level, Sarah and Luke were most excited by the adventure of it all.

Just the buying of the house was an adventure. There was the notary, the bank manager, the estate agent and the previous owners. Luke, Sarah and Luke's mother Daisy, who was staying with them for a few weeks to help out, were all in one small hot room.

Daisy wasn't managing with the heat and drama. She was desperate for a cold drink. Preferably a very long glass of blonde beer. She could practically taste it, feel the chilly glass in her hand, see the drops of condensation glistening. The white linen shirt that had seemed so smart when she put it on that morning was clinging to her arms and back, so that the skin underneath looked sausage-pink. 'Not a good look,' Daisy was thinking, 'I'm not at my most elegant.' She stood and gave a tug to her linen shorts, which were also sticking to her slim legs and had damp patches. Daisy sat again, not wanting to touch her face, which felt as if it were melting. If she touched it, there would be smudges of runny mascara trapped in the tiny wrinkles around her eyes.

She watched her son and daughter-in-law, the two so similar in the leanness of their build and sharpness of their facial features, going over the documents for the newly purchased house. They both seemed to wear the heat with ease. *Signora* Gallo, the estate agent, was running her fingers through her shoulder-length reddish hair, no longer imprisoned in a tight bun. She was impatient to have done with these English clients who failed to sign the documents properly the first time and had to be guided through the process again. An estate agent's life is a busy one and *Signora* Gallo was making it clear she didn't have the time to spend on this child-like English couple with their bare legs and dusty clothes and backpacks.

At this stage, Luke's understanding of Italian was still rudimentary, while Sarah's GCSE in Italian did not equip her for negotiating the various documents, daunting in any language—'really, I knew zero.'

They did not have the documents translated into English. This turned out to be a mistake. For all their complexity, the official documents were vague.

Sarah and Luke found out that the usual practice when buying and selling property was to declare a lower sale price than the desired one in order to pay less tax. The official paperwork would show the lower price, although in fact the estate agent would impose the higher price. Everything was carried out in cash. The notary, officious and plump, offered Luke and Sarah the choice of paying the full amount by cheque or a smaller amount with the remainder offered to the notary as cash under the table. Both the buyer and the seller must pay the notary and the estate agent.

They paid in the Italian currency at that time, *lire*. The *lira* (singular of *lire*) was the currency of Italy between 1861 (when Italy was barely a country) and 2002, but just as Luke and Sarah were buying their house, the currency was changing identity, becoming an official subunit of the euro. By 2002, Italians were using euros rather than *lire*. *Lire* were known for their excessive number of zeros—in 1999, £1.00 in British sterling was worth about 3 000.00 *lire, L3 000.*

The purchase of the house was Sarah and Luke's introduction to what could be described as a thorough approach to the law. Italy has more laws than any other European country.

The mortgage document was twenty pages, each of which had to be signed—and signed with the full set of names in the right order. But there was confusion. Luke forgot that at birth he was named Francesco Luke and not the other way around. Having signed everything Luke Francesco, he was now obliged to re-sign all the papers.

These days, Luke has a particularly relaxed view of the law in Italy. Of course, there are a lot of laws; that's because everyone breaks them, so new ones have to be made. And then they just get broken again...

Daisy was keener and keener to get out of the cramped office and have that cold beer. *Signora* Gallo's relentless hair smoothing was getting on her nerves. Luke was speaking Italian, being cooperative, why was the woman being so... rude?

Later in the café, Daisy was downing her beer and Sarah and Luke were sipping their espressos—*beer at this time in the morning, seriously Mum*? Daisy didn't care. Cold blonde beer was what was required after *Signora* G and all that paper signing. They were excited, but their excitement, especially Sarah's, was edged with an hysterical nervousness. They'd done it—smacked down those millions of *lire* for what? A dilapidated semi-ruin perched on the top of a mountain in the rural landscape of Piedmont, a region they hardly knew. She and Luke looked at each other. Both had fair complexions, now lightly tanned, and blue eyes. Sarah's were particularly blue, intensely blue in this close-to-midday sun. They had managed to keep their cool in the lawyer's office, but now it was as if their bodies were allowing their feelings to emerge into the open in the form of rivulets of sweat, snaking slowly down their cheeks. Sarah leaned over towards Luke to catch a drop with her finger.

'Well, we've done it.'

'*Si sicuramente ce l'abbiamo!*' (We certainly have!) said Luke, grinning broadly. He is not a naturally ebullient person, but his grin took in not just his wife and his mother, sitting opposite, but everyone seated on the café terrace and, indeed, the town square.

What on earth lay ahead? How would their lives turn out?

The first few days

They had decided to buy the house after one viewing. The house belonged to them now, and they to it. When they had first seen it, they were overwhelmed by the views, by the scents, by the location. This time, as they approached the house, all three silent, caught up in their own thoughts, apprehensive, excited and scared, they could remember few details of what the house looked like. What indeed had they handed over their savings for? What would they find?

The house was oddly well equipped, not with functioning toilet, heat, electricity or kitchen, but the personal effects of the long-since departed previous owners. In this neglected building, uninhabited for about eight years, there was no electricity, but there was a fruit juicer, which they discovered in a wardrobe in one of the bedrooms upstairs.

There was no heating in the house. The estate agent had described the winters as mild and short. Not so. Luke and Sarah had wondered whether they would need heating in the winter, which as they later realised, was naïve. They were beguiled; their Italian holidays had only prepared them for sunshine and heat, maybe some rain, but never snowdrifts.

What they did not consider was the savage nature of the climate—hot summers with temperatures often over 30 degrees Celsius; cold winters with temperatures down to zero.

Everything was dank and musty, and Sarah sometimes felt overwhelmed with the smell of the past. The terracotta tiles that made up the floor sat directly on the soil, blackened with damp and dirt. As you entered on the ground floor, to the right were two small, crudely divided rooms. The first was a dining room, dominated by a large wood burning stove and exposed vent tube; a dull beige Formica dining table with matching chairs, which made Sarah feel faintly clammy; a straw mattress sofa, heaven for mice; a wooden sideboard full of cups, plates and other crockery—not all chipped—and a sewing machine.

This led to the narrow kitchen. Two well-used cookers, long-congealed streaks of grease embedded in their sides, were lined up against one wall, fuelled by a small gas cylinder.

At the back of one of the cookers, the mice had nested. 'Another smell—mice urine.' Sarah laughed and wrinkled her nose. She wasn't laughing when the smell attacked her senses as they explored the house properly in the first few days after the purchase. Her heart was sinking under the weight of the renovation work she and Luke were facing. Not that she admitted it, even to herself.

The kitchen also contained an ancient washing machine that drained into a ceramic sink perched under a small window, the glass smeared with the long-spilt blood of dead insects. On the other side of the window stood a tall wooden dresser, full of towels and linens and hazelnut shells. (Daisy thought the eaters of the hazelnuts were rats, but they turned out to be *ghiri*, 'a combination of a rat and a squirrel,' according to Luke, although the dictionary translation is dormouse or gopher. This was one of many discoveries they made. The *ghiri* are troublesome little creatures with a penchant for living in, and munching on, the roof. But Sarah and Luke are tolerant household companions. 'It's their environment, we're invading it.')

Some of the towels were quite threadbare and stiff with neglect and dried mouse urine, but some of the table linens retained their old-fashioned beauty—edged with hand-made lace and embroidered in cotton silk with tiny flowers in yellows and greens, pinks and blues.

There was simply stuff everywhere—family photos, magazines, sewing paraphernalia, lots of pictures of the Madonna in different poses with the baby Jesus. A crusty piece of soap and a dingy towel waited by the sink, plus two hot water bottles ready for the night. This gave Sarah pause. She wasn't so much spooked as filled with nostalgia on behalf of the house's previous inhabitants. Luke shared her sense of the poignancy of this transfer of ownership, but also felt settled and right. This was supposed to happen.

The house had a toilet of sorts located in a derelict space at the back of the two upstairs bedrooms. It leaked, so the mains tap had to be turned on and off manually each time water was required. The problem was that the tap was downstairs in the *cantina,* the cellar, with its slimy earth floor and the occasional passing rat. It was located at the back of the house, behind the kitchen. There were no lights. The house was not yet connected—officially—to the electric grid. Dark, stinking—the cellar was not a place to linger. 'We called it the green slime floor room,' says Sarah, with a grimace.

The *cantina* was damp and dark, but just as full of the previous occupants' belongings as the rest of the house. Visible water pipes passed through the cellar. In one corner stood a rusting, ramshackle Vespa scooter, not exactly the glamorous accoutrement of so many films set in Italy, while in another, stood three huge old barrels, along with a concrete grape tank. All around, rubbish lay strewn—well fertilised by the mice and rats.

37

When they were forced to use the toilet in the house, Sarah and Daisy, tough resourceful women both, put aside their feminist principles to allow Luke to deal with the water tap in the *cantina*. Not that Luke was that keen on meeting up with the cellar rats and if anything, as the baby of his family, had become used to being protected from life's harsher realities. No longer. It was Luke's job to brave the cellar, turn on the water for the women, retreat and then enter that stinking green slime floor room again to turn it off.

They tried to time their longer toilet visits with trips into the local town. This became their routine in those first days. They quickly made friends with proprietors of the two local cafés, where they always made time for an espresso or, if Daisy were with them, beer. If their digestive habits had not been regular, they quickly became so.

There was no sewerage system in place, no septic tank. Once the water was turned on, the sewage simply dumped onto the land through the large orange plastic tube, which they couldn't help but notice on their first encounter with the house. It was attached to the toilet, ran through the cellar and emptied itself about 30cm from the back of the house. Luke and Sarah had not thought too much about where the waste landed when they first laid eyes on the house, but more about how soon they would have to install some workable waste management system.

The sewage dumped out onto the north-facing slice of land that forms a barrier between the sinuous road and the back wall of *Cascina Cannella*. This land remains permanently frozen in winter and barely supports growth, except for some very old hazelnut trees. This is known as the hazelnut grove.

*

The Madonna's dark cracked face stared down at Daisy as she lay in the slightly damp bed in the dark, waiting for sleep. They had found the picture hanging there when they were sorting out sleeping arrangements. Daisy was allocated the Madonna bedroom, while Luke and Sarah took the other one. Both bedrooms included beds, made up ready with blankets and covers tucked into the straw-filled mattresses. They even found slippers placed under the beds.

That first night imprinted itself vividly on Daisy's memory. She told her son she was quite happy to take this room, that he and Sarah should have the other one, which was brighter and more spacious.

It had been a long time since Daisy and the Virgin were on speaking terms. The bed was wide, so not at all cosy. And there was no heating in this wreck of a house perched on the top of a mountain in northern Italy. Well, there wasn't any easy way to get hot water either, so the old hot water bottles they found in the kitchen would have been of no use. Daisy was sleeping on an ancient straw-filled mattress, which might or might not have been inhabited by any number of small mammals or insects, and her goose down duvet and fresh sheets seemed a very long way away.

The Madonna was continuing to fix her dark eyes on Daisy from her exalted position on the wall opposite the bed where Daisy lay, wakeful and wanting to pee. Was she being accused of something?

'What do you want?

'Oh God I'm talking to a picture.'

She needed to pee urgently now. Luke had given her an old chamber pot, better than negotiating the cold stone stairs to the miserable cellar. Did she dare pee in front of the Virgin?

The picture was painted in sombre colours, the oils further darkened with age and dirt. How long had she been there, presiding over the long slow decay of the deserted house atop a mountain? What had happened in this room? When Luke and Sarah first arrived, they found the floor to ceiling wardrobe packed with left-behind stuff—clothes, shoes, photographs, layers of folded fabrics and wedding gifts that had never been used, but had been carefully put away. This was where they found the fruit juicer, accompanied by knives and forks, more linen tablecloths and napkins embroidered with the initials of those long-gone inhabitants. For some reason, neither of them felt able simply to dispose of the portrait of the Madonna. She had been gazing out from that bedroom wall, undisturbed, for so long.

Daisy could feel her heart speeding up in her chest, thumping against her rib cage. She was not old, but nor was she young. No one ever believed her when she said she was in her early sixties. If she was out with my mother, Daisy's senior by eleven years, people sometimes assumed they were mother and daughter. This upset my mother, also a youthful and stylish woman, and there were times when I overheard her introducing Daisy to friends with an extremely firm pre-emptive strike: 'This is my sister...' My mother didn't always escape, however. The insensitive would exclaim, 'Oh, but you look so alike, she could be your daughter.' My mother's small mouth would crimp at the corners. Nevertheless, she was devoted to her younger sister, a slightly irascible sort of devotion.

Daisy had lived alone for some years now, but always with her son close by. That was all going to change with the signing of the papers. Luke's attention was going to be focused on this house, on his new life with Sarah in Italy. Daisy hadn't really let herself think beyond this moment. But now, in the early hours of a foreign dawn in a house full of someone else's memories, she couldn't stop thinking. And the Madonna was offering no comfort. Where was she when Gino, her little Catholic shit of a husband, pissed off with her best friend? Sisterhood. Yeah right.

'It's no good, I have to go.'

She was often in the habit of talking to herself. Easy when you live alone. Back again on the lumpy lively mattress, Daisy met the Madonna's eyes. How many times did she pray to her back in those days? On her own with three children and terrified. She pushed herself off the bed, scooped up the covers and made a dash for it into the refuge of Luke and Sarah's room.

And that's where she stayed. The three of them ended up sleeping together in the same room that entire first week.

*

Apart from the weather, there was a more significant aspect to their swiftly taken decision to buy the house.

Cascina Cannella was located next to an abandoned house with a 'for sale' sign.

Luke and Sarah never even considered what this might mean. Little did they know that this great adventure they were embarking on would become a struggle, not only to establish a real and viable life in Italy, but also to establish how much they were willing to sacrifice.

But on that day and at that moment when they stood looking at the vineyard on the hillside, Sarah and Luke had no idea the trouble the abandoned house next door would cause them and how they would be forced to look deep inside themselves for the strength to hold onto the dream.

CHAPTER 3 *bis*

Tales of the Toilet

At least Sarah and Luke had a toilet on which to sit. Luxury. When we bought our house in France back in 1992—two rooms and a shed, laid out in a line—there was no toilet at all. There was, however, running water and a thunderbox in the shed that stood next to the stone exterior of the house on the site of what had once been another room, but was now a ruin. The house was originally a Normandy *longère*, a long house, but it wasn't long any more. Only one wall of the ruin was left standing, precariously upright, a triangle of stone pointing to the sky. In the shed, illuminated by daylight coming through the wooden slats, was a tall hollow wooden box with a bottom-shaped hole cut in the top on which you sat. It was a high box, difficult for the children to clamber up on satisfactorily. This wasn't much of a problem, as our daughter (aged two) was using a potty and our son (aged four) welcomed the chance to become feral and busied himself in the long grass.

The thunderbox had to be emptied periodically into a hole that had to be dug and to be big enough to accommodate not just us, but also visiting family. Like Luke and Sarah, we got to know a lot of the local cafés.

To keep things smelling sweet(ish), we sloshed a lot of pink disinfectant into the box. It was generally stored next to the toilet. There was the occasional mix-up in the system and other things might be stored there too, if you were in a hurry. Barbecue lighter fluid, for example.

In those days, a lot of people smoked, including my mother and my husband, H. Where better to have a quiet cigarette and a moment of contemplation than in the shed? You could leave the door open and gaze out at the cows in the field that belonged to the farm next door, thinking pastoral thoughts. And then you could dispose of your fag in the obvious place. On one occasion, H decided it was his turn to disinfect and duly poured thick shiny pink liquid into the box. It was only as he was turning to chuck the remains of his cigarette into the pit he became aware of the strong scent of lighter fuel. He still had hold of the glowing cigarette end. He hopped quickly off the box, scrambled out of the shed and threw the butt into the cow field before breaking out into a seriously cold sweat.

We found no fine linens or fancy china when we took possession of our French house, but we did find something extraordinary. This was the house's crowning accoutrement without doubt—the giant sink, shower hose and bidet combo that had been left behind. Located in the one bedroom, it was all singing, all dancing and made of iridescent orange plastic. We loved it and it served us well for those first years. The children even used the bidet as a sneaky nighttime place to pee, too scared to venture out to the shed, even if the thunderbox had been quite quickly replaced with a toilet. It still had to be flushed with a pail of water each time it was used. And by the time we acquired a proper plumbed in toilet and a septic tank, the peeing-in-the-bidet habit was ingrained.

CHAPTER 4
A magical place

Their first real summer at *Cascina Cannella*, while it was still a 'holiday house,' was given over to exploring the area and planning the renovations. There was also time to spend in the pursuit of wine. Luke was scouting out new suppliers, keen to add to his growing collection of Italian wines. Sarah often talks about the difficulty Luke has in saying no to more wine—in the sense of acquiring it rather than drinking it himself.

'Do you drink a lot of your own product, Luke? Not the wine you make, but the wine you buy in?' I ask one evening, laughing. I'm quite interested to know how much he drinks. If you love wine, how do you regulate how much you drink and how often you drink it?

'Of course I do.' Luke is indignant, in his quiet way. He never raises his voice or seems to get irritated. He is both confident and modest.

'I buy it knowledgeably, hopefully. Even if I'm selling it at the lowest end of the market, when it doesn't really matter, where people don't really know anything and want to pay the lowest price, I always get it from the producers I know.'

'So you taste it all?'

'I wouldn't supply a bottle that I didn't know,' he says, his blue eyes narrowing.

I think that answers my question, although I have the feeling I will never again choose the very cheap wine on Luke's list for fear of going down in his estimation. I am a wine snob, after all, especially in front of my younger cousin. Luke is a student of Italian wine, believes firmly that wine produced in Italy is the best in the world and argues his case with conviction, even with those for whom France continues to set the ultimate standard—i.e. me.

(Interestingly, it was thought that the wine regarded as Italy's king of wines, the world-renowned Barolo, was first created in its present form by a Frenchman, oenologist *Monsieur* Louis Oudart, back in the mid-nineteenth century. He was hired by Camillo Benso, *Conte di Cavour* (Count of Cavour), known as the architect of Italian unity and mayor of Grinzane Cavour in the Barolo area. The family French wine versus Italian wine debate continues.)

I am curious about where Luke's passion for Italian wine came from.

'Michael (Luke's older brother) says it's because of him.'

Sarah doesn't agree. She is pursing her lips and frowning.

'No, don't shake your head like that,' Luke rebukes her playfully. 'It's true. Michael used to drink *Lungarotti rubesco* and he said I loved it so much that my interest started from there.' (The Lungarotti name belongs to the wine produced from vineyards in Torgiano and Montefalco in Umbria, which is below the Tuscany region, about half way down the boot of Italy.)

Luke and Michael have an easy relationship and when the extended family gets together, they'll come into the room, shoulder to shoulder, wearing dark glasses and the kind of well-tailored shirts some English men (Brexit supporters?) might shun, fearful of diluting their masculinity. They will be discussing something *sotto voce*, as if setting up a deal. Someone in the room will hum the theme from the *Godfather*. Luke and Michael don't appear to be bothered by the stereotyping. I think they love it.

Luke says his interest in Italian wine developed 'very, very slowly at the beginning.' In reality, his was a precocious interest.

'I remember there's a picture of the very first wine rack I had in the house where I lived after university and it had just twelve bottles in it. But if I look back and study that picture they were good wines,' he muses, not in a self-satisfied way, but as if he is surprised at his youthful expertise. He was not exactly a beer-swilling student then, getting hammered with the lads. I don't think he realises his behaviour was unusual.

'At university, I drank wine my Dad gave me. I remember he got hold of some German wine—quite good German white wine—from a supplier, and he used to give us a few bottles. I'd drink that, or Lambrusco.'

'You weren't down the off licence buying Hirondelle then?' This was the cheapest wine you could get when I was a student.

Luke doesn't laugh, but ponders the question, as if it were serious.

'No, I don't think I did that. Once my interest started, it took off very quickly.'

'You were young.' I say this almost like an accusation. How could a student be that sophisticated?

'No, I was in my very early twenties.'

So, yes, very young then.

*

Luke's nose must have led him to Piedmont, in particular to the hills of the Langhe. A famous Barolo wine is produced here from the Nebbiolo grape—*nebbia* means fog and, indeed, the hills of the Langhe are the perfect place for fog to linger and encourage the ripening of the Nebbiolo grape.

Piedmont is one of the great wine-growing regions of the country. More than half of its 700 square kilometres (170,000 acres) of vineyards are registered with DOC designations—*Denominazione di Origine Controllata*—which guarantee the quality of the wine, requiring that it is produced within a specified region and using defined methods. Many of the wines produced in Piedmont hold the highest designation, DOCG—*Denominazione di Origine Controllata e Garantita*—indicating the wine's greater quality.

Other indigenous grape varieties include the reds: Barbera, Dolcetto, Freisa, Grignolino and Brachetto. The most commonly grown white grape of Piedmont is the Moscato. It is this grape that grows in Sarah and Luke's vineyard, a green grape that changes to golden yellow as it ripens. Moscato grapes taste exactly like the Moscato wine you can buy—the wine is sweet, fizzy (*spumante*) and 5.5% alcohol.

Most of the winemaking in Piedmont takes place in the provinces of Cuneo, Asti and Alessandria. Prominent figures in Italy's history, such as Camillo Benso, Count of Cavour (Barolo enthusiast) and Giuseppe Garibaldi, owned vineyards in Piedmont. Both played a significant part in the unification of Italy—the process known as the *Risorgimento*. The punitively high tariffs imposed on the export of *Piemontese* wines to areas of northern Italy under Austrian control may have played a part in the revolutions of 1848-1849.

The majority of the *Cascina Cannella* vines are around fifty years old and are perfect to make *Moscato passito*—a deep, intensely yellow-coloured wine, 13% alcohol. The grapes dry easily on the vines and turn a deep yellow-orange as they shrink to the size of raisins, becoming ever sweeter and more flavourful. New vines, planted annually to replace any old dead vines, produce tight bunches of grapes, while the old vines produce tiny grapes in open bunches.

When they first arrived, Sarah and Luke were overwhelmed—in a delighted way—about the vineyard. It has almost become a cliché of the dream. A lot of people, of small means and great, manage to find themselves a home from home that gives them respite from their regular lives. They buy or rent a caravan or a tent, sail a boat, purchase a house in the country, maybe a house in another country. Not many end up as owners of a real vineyard. But it's not all lazy days in the sun, sipping on a pleasant Moscato d'Asti while you contemplate the hills and valleys rolling themselves out before you, in shimmery green velvet furrows. Grape vines require considerable care to maintain and are most demanding.

*

After their first *vendemmia* (grape harvest), Sarah and Luke were on their way back to the house in the UK, which was feeling less and less like home, as the Italian house was becoming harder and harder to leave.

'We were so thrilled to have our own grapes, from our very own vineyard—we piled them high into an open crate and balanced them on top of the usual boxes and boxes of Luke's wine,' Sarah remembers. They had also packed a bag of large, fresh porcini mushrooms for a last taste of Italy back in the UK. The porcini were packed next to Sarah's feet in the path of a cold air vent to keep them fresh—both feet and mushrooms.

However, Sarah and Luke got more than a lovely flavourful reminder of Italy. As the famous wine-growing areas of France flashed by—Burgundy, Champagne—Sarah became aware that things were starting to move. She felt slightly itchy—oh yes, an ant on the bare shoulder, brush it away… But then more appeared. Luke started to scratch. Another ant… Sarah looked behind her to check the cargo —a crowd, a mob, an *army* of ants was streaming into the car from the pile of beautiful Moscato grapes, so proudly displayed.

Sarah leaned to check on the mushrooms beside her feet. Oh, the bag appeared to be moving. It turned out that the cold air vent had not been too effective. Warmth had persuaded a bunch of worms to emerge, blinking into the light from their mushroom cave.

'It was one of those memorable journeys. We made so many of them, but this one stood out. And it went on being memorable as the ants refused to leave the car even when we were back in the UK.' Sarah shudders slightly.

*

Piedmont is something of a secret to non-Italians. When people chat about going to Italy on holiday, or imagine the heat and light of an Italian landscape, they tend to think of Tuscany or a Mediterranean resort, of the decaying glamour of Venice or Rome and its immense history, Florence and its architecture... the list continues. Italy is so studded with cultural and topographical jewels. They probably don't think automatically of Piedmont (unless they are in the wine business, perhaps).

Piedmont is different—not as well known to tourists, but somewhere country life hasn't changed much at all for years and local people live according to established traditions. It is surrounded on three sides by the Alps and the Apennines—as the name suggests, it lies at the foot, *piede,* of the mountain, *montagna.* The town of Alba and the surrounding Langhe hills are protected by UNESCO World Heritage status. The area is celebrated not only for its wine, but also for its white truffles (in contrast to the black truffles found further south).

When Sarah and Luke first bought the house, it demanded much of them, physically and mentally. Apart from the clearing out, the cleaning, the work necessary to make it habitable, they spent hours thinking about what building work they would need, what were their goals, how did they wish the house and its land to look and behave. What, in short, did they want from this crumbling object of their affections?

Their house, the house that seduced them, is in the hilly Langhe area, where buildings are constructed from local stone In the hours left over (not many) when they weren't tending to the house's needs, they took delight in exploring the Langhe, *their* area. The roads twist and turn through small villages where the houses are solidly built, the walls of a thickness to defend against the heat, sometimes painted in dusty creams, dim ochres and dull pinks, all set against the intense blue of the summer sky. For when they were first roaming, it was always summer. They discovered sleepy family restaurants with set menus, meat and pasta; they discovered isolated houses, sometimes of mansion proportions, in the hills. These grand houses might belong to foreigners, northern Europeans or Americans rich enough to maintain such a property ready for the occasional visit; unexpected luxury in the spare and hard-worked hills.

At every bend, they came on a different view of the slopes and vineyards. And they found places to walk along sandy paths through shady groves, not always inviting them up a mountainside, but allowing them to stroll comfortably through the bowery hazelnut trees. They were enthralled by the contrasts in the *Piemontese* countryside, the mountains and hills, the plains and valleys. The Novara plains, rich agricultural land where the rice crop thrives, are watery and alive with mosquitoes, fed by the river Po, the longest river in the whole of Italy (652 kilometres). On its way to the Adriatic Sea, the Po collects all the waters within the semicircle of mountains. Springs crisscross the great Padan plain, supplying fresh water to the rivers and a network of irrigation canals.

This wide-open grandeur was less appealing to them than the quiet hills, where they stumbled on secluded places of breathless beauty. This is where small local wineries hide their secrets.

And this is where Luke and Sarah fetched up, almost by accident.

As they discovered more of the landscape and its quirks, they became increasingly convinced that this place—which, as they say, chose them—had the most charm and beauty. Farmers may no longer use bulls to plough the fields, dirt roads may have been tarmacked (although not all), woodland may have been cut in certain areas, but there is a timelessness to the Langhe. It is magical.

*

Luke and Sarah found themselves slipping into this rural life, essentially unchanged over the years. They themselves were becoming part of Piedmont's living history, inserting themselves into the everyday patterns of the neighbourhood, becoming real *Piemontese*.

One witness to the old, but still recognisable way of life in Piedmont is Annalisa Colombara, a native, now an artist living and working in London, England. She is a tall and imposing woman, in her sixties, with a shock of dark curly hair, still the darkest brown with only whispers of grey at the edges. She speaks flawless English, but with an Italian lilt. She carries a sense of drama. She could not be mistaken for anything but an Italian woman; so expressive are her hands, voice, movements.

Annalisa talks about her childhood growing up in Novara, in the neighbourhood where Luke and Sarah have settled. The family used to buy their wine from such villages as La Morra, Canelli and Santo Stefano Belbo—wines like Barolo, Barbera, Barbaresco, Dolcetto, as well as white wines, such as Moscato di Canelli.

'Barely forty years ago, children would be offered Moscato to drink when they went on school trips to neighbouring farms because it was a rare occasion when the water was drinkable. In church, you would see rows of wine bottles standing on the altar.' Annalisa chuckles fruitily.

Her father, born in Novara in 1912, used to buy his wine for around L2,000 a bottle/£1.00 in the 1970s. These days, Luke sells a bottle of (vintage) Barolo for anything from to £35.00 to £130.00 or more.

51

'Dad was a maker of Gorgonzola cheese. His name was on the label, N. Colombara. Look, here.' Annalisa is digging out an example from a tin of treasures. The label's original colours were black and orange, but they are faded and grainy now. You can still see the name clearly though.

'There is a story—I can't say if it's true or not—that Winston Churchill asked the Royal Air Force not to bomb Novara in World War II, because the region was the principal producer of this cheese. And, apparently, Novara was never bombed,' says Annalisa, grinning.

She has stayed in England through a variety of circumstances—marriage to an English fellow artist, work, friends. Her daughter, born in the UK, is also an artist of growing renown. Known as Joy BC, she fashions intricate jewellery from precious metals. Somehow, Annalisa has never managed to return to her beloved Piedmont, but she is able to conjure its scents and tastes through cooking some of the dishes she remembers from her early life in the hills of the Langhe. She makes *bagna cauda*, for instance, a sauce made from garlic, cream and anchovies in which you dip vegetables. Or she whips up *il fritto misto Piemontese,* deep fried foods, such as different meats or vegetables or sweet things, like fruit or biscuits. And while the French have their cognac, the Italians have their grappa, a powerful distilled liqueur. Annalisa will take a small glass of grappa on occasion.

Annalisa sometimes goes into her garden (she lives on the ground floor of a terraced house in south east London) and picks courgette flowers, dips them in flour and beaten egg, then fries them quickly in a mixture of oil and butter until light, crisp and delicious. You eat them sitting at her kitchen table, surrounded not only by Annalisa's own paintings, but the favourite objects she has collected—a hand-painted teacup, small silver teaspoons, copper pans next to the old-fashioned gas cooker with its overhead grill. There is always a large vase of unexpected flowers on the table—hydrangeas, peonies, branches from the apricot tree, *'an offering to the ancestors'*—all grown in her tiny, perfect London garden.

You might well be in Piedmont, because England has disappeared.

*

And fill all fruit with
ripeness to the core;
To swell the gourd,
and plump the hazel shells
With a sweet kernel

Keats, 'To Autumn'

You can't talk about Piedmont without considering the hazelnut, *nocciola*. This is the birthplace of Nutella, the chocolate-hazelnut spread made by Ferrero, which inspires addiction in some and disgust in others. The Celts believed hazelnuts were associated with wisdom and poetic inspiration—the Gaelic word for the nuts is *cno*, while the word for wisdom is *cnocach*. Annalisa says that Gaelic was one of the dialects spoken in a neighbourhood about twenty miles away from the valley in which she grew up. Her own parents spoke another local dialect, while inhabitants of other valleys spoke *Occitan*, derived from the *Langue d'Oc*, an old French language spoken by people in the Languedoc region of France.

(*Occitan* is still spoken today in parts of France. When I lived down in Lozère in the Midi I was invited for a Sunday lunch featuring *boudin*, black pudding made from pig's blood. This *boudin* was from my host's pig who died from a cut throat, so that the blood could drain directly into a bucket. The slaughter took place metres from where I sat. I'm unsure what disturbed me most, the *boudin* or my friends chatting away in an unfamiliar dialect when I had only just got the hang of standard French. Both stomach and head were queasily bamboozled.)

An ancient Celtic story, one of those magical tales that seems to accord with Sarah's sense of the magical in the Langhe, concerns nine hazel trees growing around a sacred pool. Salmon ate the nuts that fell into the water and absorbed the wisdom—and the more bright spots that appeared on their skin, the more nuts they had eaten and the wiser they were.

*

Cascina Cannella has its hazelnut grove, but this hazelnut grove is a sorry strip of land behind the house, with mostly barren trees bereft of the tasty fat fruits of Keats's imagination. No wise salmon and poetical hazelnuts.

While Sarah and Luke were still shuttling back and forth to *Cascina Cannella*, still living their daily lives in England, all they thought about were the building tasks that lay ahead of them, the clearing of land, the establishing of a habitable and, at some point, comfortable, home from home.

Little did they know when they settled in the misty beauty of the Langhe hills how significant this narrow strip would become.

CHAPTER 4 *bis*

Tasty things that Annalisa remembers from her early life from the hills of the Langhe:

Bagna cauda
You make creamy garlic and anchovy sauce and then dip your vegetables in it:
200 ml olive oil
5-6 cloves of garlic, crushed
10-12 anchovies, drained and chopped
100g butter
Put the oil in a pan, add the garlic and cook until soft, add the anchovies and cook over a low heat until they dissolve. Don't let the garlic burn. Add the butter; let it melt, then serve warm. The sauce is best kept simmering and warm. Choose any veg to dip into the sauce —celery, peppers, carrots, cauliflower, mushrooms, artichoke hearts, turnips, fennel, spring onions, boiled potatoes and so on. And bread, of course.

This traditional sauce can also be made with milk, leaving out the butter:

Heat the garlic in about a litre of milk, first bringing the mixture to the boil and then letting it simmer for about an hour. Pour off the milk and crush the garlic with a fork. Heat the garlic with the oil and the anchovies until the anchovies have dissolved.

Grappa
Grappa is a powerful liqueur, made by distilling discarded grape pulp, skins, stalks, seeds and stems that are a by-product of the winemaking process, known as pomace. It was originally made as a way of using up these waste products.

CHAPTER 5
One foot in Italy

Sarah and Luke continued repeatedly to break the law. The house had to be cleaned. Rubbish to be cleared out. There were days of cleaning and clearing and filling large plastic sacks. They had to do this on every visit. Luke would keep expanding the radius of his movements in search of available refuse bins. But they did not know that this was all highly illegal at the time. In fact, they didn't know much. They did a lot of illegal things without realising.

In amongst all that cleaning and clearing, that dirty work, there were discoveries that cheered them. Like the homemade rag rug Daisy found and took home with her to England to clean up and install in her kitchen. Or some of the intact china and well-preserved linens, edged with handmade lace, folded and stored. And Sarah, ever the perfectionist, always insisted on putting cups and saucers away in the damp cupboards. It was as if she needed to have some measure of control over their surroundings. She was determined to leave the Italian house as clean and tidy as it was possible to make a rundown old building, despite the fact that she knew everything was just going to get dirty again, particularly once the builders started work.

Daisy remembers Sarah washing all the crockery.

'Stupid really,' Sarah murmurs when she hears Daisy say this.

'It was just a matter of saying, "This is mine and it's got to stay safe,"' says Daisy now. She thinks this was Sarah's small rebellion against a loss of control. This feeling increased when the builders arrived. They behaved according to their own rules.

Sarah continued doggedly to persist in putting cups and saucers away in the damp cupboards.

*

For around three years, Luke and Sarah shuttled back and forth, between work in the UK and the dream in Italy. It became a routine. They adapted quickly to the 860-mile drive to *Cascina Cannella*. They would take the Eurotunnel, then hightail it along the fantastic *autoroutes* and *autostrada* of France and Italy to their house. Going to the house was always thrilling, but also made Luke and Sarah apprehensive, even if they didn't always express that to each other.

What would they find this time? The house was unprotected, standing alone as it did amid vine-covered hillsides, next to an empty property, still unsold. It was a place of shelter for all kinds of wildlife, maybe some human wildlife too. The house would take on its own life when Luke and Sarah weren't there, shifting and settling into itself. The slime floor of the *cantina* (cellar) would thicken and grow greener. The taps would drip—the droplets adding to the rust stain in the basin, dripping regularly, unheard, uninterrupted. A flake of buttermilk plaster might fall from a wall. A wooden door might slowly creak open. Rust would continue to creep along a metal handle.

Mice would re-establish their presence too, taking up residence in nooks and crannies, accompanied always by their stash of hazel nuts. They, and others, would leave a trail of dung and urine and shells, while curling up in anything soft—a feather pillow, still with tasty morsels attached to the feathers, easy enough to gain entrance, to nibble into the fabric of the cover. They would give birth in the straw mattress seat of the couch, make a good home for the small, naked baby mice to grow, feed, develop hair, leave home to start their own colonies elsewhere, in some other pillow, some other mattress…

Insects burrowed into beams, dug channels through soft wood. Spiders wove webs in the corners of rooms, criss-crossed stone walls with the taut silk lattice, trapped flies and other food. Rolled them up into savoury little bundles for later.

The earth went through its seasons, hardened under the piles of winter snow, froze in the winter temperatures. Stood hard like iron. As the snows melted, the temperatures rose, the crumbs of the soil relaxed, expanded, said hello to warmth. Then summer, and the baking of the earth, its soil turning into a landscape of jagged edges, furrows and waterless ground.

It seemed to Sarah and Luke, that in some way the animals were entitled to make *Cascina Cannella* their home too when the human occupants weren't there. How selfish, how blinkered, to suppose all life stopped because humans weren't there to witness it. They thought about the weather a lot too. Still living their life in southern England, they checked what the day would hold, then the forecast for their patch of Piedmont. Is it freezing there today? Or is the spring warmth starting to unfurl the grape vines?

*

It wasn't just the animals making their home in *Cascina Cannella*. The builders working on site were not just working there. Sarah and Luke didn't understand this at first. There was a lot they didn't understand.

'We know that the first building team lived in our house,' Sarah says one day when we are sitting at the stone table in the garden, eating homemade cake, seamed with the red juice of summer fruits, for our breakfast. It is not just me and Sarah enjoying the cake. Daisy is sitting with us after abandoning her attempt to finish the last few pages of her book in sunny seclusion. She is way too curious to know what we're talking about. Also, she wants cake. This cake is good.

Sarah is talking quite matter-of-factly, but her tone is crisp and it is clear the memory still rankles, even though she has turned it into an anecdote.

'They put their finger in my marmalade.' We all giggle. 'Obviously, they didn't like the English marmalade. They just left it to go mouldy.'

At this stage, builders had already started renovation. The house was full of holes. The windows were holes, the doors were only held closed with planks of wood. There was no place to hide anything. Luke, meanwhile, was continuing to seek new wine producers. He was keen to try new wines, thinking about expanding his range, introducing more people to the joys of Italian varieties. One day he might be able to leave the day job and devote himself full-time to learning every fascinating detail about Italian wine and to becoming a trusted wine merchant to his own clientele. For now, though, he was faced with the tough choice of what wine to leave behind when the time came to head back to England. He realised it was not going to be possible to take the ever increasing number of bottles with them and still squeeze themselves into the car. He needed a place to store some of the cases. Sarah, ever practical, was worried the builders would take the wine.

Luke wasn't bothered.

'Wine's like water around here, it's so cheap, it's not worth them taking it,' he reassured Sarah, without an inkling of doubt.

'No Luke, we should store some of the more expensive stuff in a locked wardrobe. We could store the other bottles, the less expensive ones, in various cupboards.'

When Luke looked dubious, she pushed him a bit. 'Look, the cupboards are in rooms where they won't be doing a lot of work, so they should be safe.'

The planned work involved sandblasting ceilings to clean plaster off the vaulted brickwork and reveal the old oak beams. This didn't seem like a lot of work to Sarah, which gives an indication of her exceptional determination, considering the scale of the project ahead. She is not a dabbler. Brushing paint on walls is not a lot of work, grouting is more work, stripping a pine floor with a sander is serious work. Sandblasting ceilings to get rid of decades of old plaster is an *enormous* amount of work.

Sarah thought of everything, as she usually did. They covered all the cupboards in thick plastic. They would be back in five months…

However, during their absence, there was a change of plan—as it turns out, not that unusual an occurrence in the renovating of *Cascina Cannella*. The second floor could not be strengthened from below. The old tiles in these rooms had to be taken up. Sarah was determined to keep all the original features that they could, including the floor tiles. She loved the look of them—their faded coppery patina. And she loved the feel of them—the textured surface of fine cracks and fissures. These rooms, of course, were the rooms in which the cupboards were located and where the wine was stored. How would the builders move the cupboards? But Luke and Sarah weren't that concerned. Life was busy. Italy was a long way away.

Five months later, in the wonderful month of May— spring unfolding, warmth during the daytime, the vines coming back to life—they arrived back at *Cascina Cannella*, full of their usual slightly anxious excitement.

They discovered what had happened to the cupboards.

One had been physically lifted into another room, whilst a couple of other larger wardrobes were scattered about in pieces. And the wine? Luke looked for it in vain. He found a few bottles here and there in the boxes he had carefully filled and stored.

Then he searched in the locked wardrobe—still locked —and found a few bottles dotted about in the previously full boxes.

'The builders obviously managed to unlock the wardrobe, take out the wine they wanted and then lock it up again—they thought we wouldn't notice,' says Sarah, raising her eyebrows and only half smiling. She is trusting and doesn't like to be made a fool of.

Luke did a head count. A total of thirty-seven bottles of wine were missing and a couple of bottles of grappa.

Later, wandering about the house, a bit dazed, frustrated, unnerved, sad, Luke found empty bottles here and there. He picked each one up, looked at the label, remembered where he had managed to source that bottle.

'The builders obviously knew their wine,' he says, drily. Only the better labels had been selected and joyously quaffed.

*

In addition to the animals making themselves at home (totally within their rights; humans had disturbed them, after all), and the builders (beyond cheeky), the locals also continued to treat the property as communal.

During those first years after Sarah and Luke bought the house, there was no official locked gate, nor barriers to their house and land. Just because it had been bought didn't mean the habits of local people were going to change. Not long after they purchased the house, they were having lunch in the front yard—actually, a dirt patch in front of a falling-down outbuilding, open to the weather—when they heard voices. Three women and a boy were strolling around the house talking and gesticulating loudly. They ignored Luke and Sarah, not appearing to notice them at all, and passed through the courtyard and down through the vineyards, obviously taking their customary short cut.

On another occasion, there was a knock on the door from a lady eating cherries from the garden, wanting to tell them how lovely the cherries were (likely a pretext to see who was living there). Then there was the neighbour who walked around the house with a woman, whom they later found out was his sister, picked up a ladder next to the hayloft and walked off with it. Some fifteen minutes later, he brought the ladder back, after using it to adjust one of his shutters. Did he know he was being watched? (And would Luke and Sarah ever watch him with such benign bemusement in the future?)

From Sarah's notes:

Summers would be an endless supply of fresh fruit. Once one glut had been bottled, frozen or made into numerous desserts, the next would appear.

(This reminds me of a children's story in which the plum tree in the garden continues to produce giant juicy purple plums season after season. The family dutifully uses them up—eating and bottling and canning—but they never manage to use up the season's fruit before the next growing season is upon them. They grow fatter and fatter…)

Our first batch of cherries was a very embarrassing experience. We had collected a bucket of cherries and were sitting happily outside in the sun, de-pipping. They were juicy and Luke had decided to disrobe down to his boxers and I had just let the juices splash where they landed. Luke had gone into the kitchen and was merrily stewing cherries, while I was washing the sticky table, when we had unexpected visitors—this was, after all a Sunday. It's a tradition, one of many in Italy we were to discover, to visit people wearing your very best Sunday clothes.

Three smartly dressed people arrived in our garden, to find me splattered in juice, hosing down a table. I quickly muttered something about my husband and dashed into the house. Luke, of course, was also not suitably dressed to meet people, so quickly located some trousers and a t-shirt. He talked to them outside, while I hid. Then I heard the door. He had brought them inside! He called for me to meet them. But I hadn't changed. I crept downstairs. Who were these people? Luke did not explain and I just smiled and shook their hands. Turned out that the girl wanted English lessons and the father worked on the roads. The girl wasn't too put off by this cherry splattered woman and I ended up teaching her English over four months.

*

Luke and Sarah lived in a world of divided loyalties during those first three years, with nothing feeling quite real, as if their proper life were somewhere else. Both were travelling a lot for work, in the UK and continental Europe. They had to concentrate on making a living. They had to focus on their social life, family life, house, garden, the cats. They found themselves emotionally scattered, wanting to be wholehearted about daily life, but feeling stretched and always, always aware of the house on the mountain biding its time, waiting for their return. It was still a holiday place, a second home, a luxury, but the idea of making it their permanent home was fermenting in the heart of their relationship.

The sixteen-hour journey grew shorter and shorter in their minds as they became more experienced in finding a comfortable sleeping position inside the car. The one who wasn't driving would fall asleep within minutes of resting their head on the pillow, while the driver whose shift it was would drive into the night for the next three-hour stint.

While they were still in this commuting stage between Italy and England, Sarah in particular was continuing to live in the present. Luke had never had doubts about his real aim in life—to live in Italy fulltime. But Sarah—she was a different case.

Some ten or so years later, we are sitting in the garden at the stone table with our morning espressos and Daisy asks Sarah how she started to think that she could do it, move to Italy. What prompted her to let her mind even entertain that possibility? Was it the state of the Italian house?

63

They are trying to bring back the reality of that time when it had dawned on Daisy that her son might leave England for good.

Sarah thinks for a moment, chewing tentatively on her bottom lip.

'I really don't think I thought. I don't think we had any of those considerations. We didn't think, consciously, about what we were taking on, how long it would take. No idea at all.'

This is a touch disingenuous. Luke never made any secret of his ambition to live in Italy. But his love for Sarah is such that he always knew it would, ultimately, have to be her decision.

When they were buying the house, Sarah asked the estate agent, *Signora* Gallo, how much she thought it would cost to renovate *Cascina Cannella*. It was an impossible question.

'Of course, she could have no idea. She didn't know what we wanted. Nor did we.'

*

You will remember that when Luke and Sarah first laid eyes on *Cascina Cannella*, in its decaying beauty, surrounded by too tall trees and overgrown vegetation, there was one thing that escaped their notice—the *For Sale* sign, half hidden in the undergrowth.

The sign belonged to a large and rather forbidding house, standing just to the side and front of *Cascina Cannella*. Tall, facing towards the narrow road, its concrete-clad back wall loomed over the driveway that led to the original entrance of *Cascina Cannella*. A one-storey square-roofed annexe squatted at its back, so that the structure looked like a prison compound, lacking only the lookout post and stalag light. Rampant undergrowth acted as camouflage, concealing the extent of the building. It had been derelict since 1988. That was about to change.

Just as Sarah and Luke were happily heading towards their house, worrying only about mice and other intruders, so the derelict building next door was beginning its reawakening. After years of standing empty, it was going to be occupied. They had no inkling of this development. They were still in the honeymoon period, not quite believing they had done this momentous thing—bought a house in a country they loved—but knew only from holidays and the stories they had been told.

There was a two-metre-wide piece of land stretching around the back of *Cascina Cannella,* holding it in a close embrace. Sarah and Luke had a document dating back to 1952, which stated they owned these two metres.

But ownership of this narrow hazelnut grove, which barely supports growth and separates *Cascina Cannella* from the road, was going to become a matter of dispute.

*

Sarah answered the phone, but quickly passed it to Luke. The caller was speaking rapidly in Italian and Sarah was still at the stage where she panicked when she had to speak, or more importantly, understand a foreign language on the phone. She had been studying Italian—as much as she could with all her other commitments—but it was still basic. Luke listened intently, his forehead creased with the effort of trying to understand. His Italian was more advanced than Sarah's, but not so advanced he could comfortably cope with rapid speech over the telephone, without visual clues.

It was *Signor* Pozzi, one of the builders.

'It's got to be some problem with the roof,' Sarah thought, as she fidgeted anxiously next to Luke, obviously having difficulty understanding *Signor* P.

'*Scusi? Come?*' he kept repeating, obviously not understanding. He was making animated hand gestures, a sure sign of his discomfiture. Luke was normally so calm and self-contained.

Eventually, he put the phone down and turned to Sarah.

'We've got a problem,' he said.

It seemed the neighbour—what neighbour?—was complaining about the overhang of the new roof, that it was greater than before the work started.

'I don't understand, what overhang? Where?'

'Apparently, it's the overhang at the back of the house, the bit of the roof that sticks out over the hazelnut grove.'

'But I thought that was *our* land?' Sarah said, confused. 'And anyway, what neighbour? Has the house next door been sold?'

'You know as much as I do,' said Luke.

*

It had been a long journey in the car down through the length of France and across the border into Northwestern Italy. This was to be even more of a working visit than usual—that business with the roof. Luke and Sarah had perked up on the *autostrada* out of necessity because of the creative lane changing that the other drivers were engaging in. Whoever was driving on this stretch—and it was usually Luke as he had the temperament—the other one had to stay awake to offer encouragement and keep an eye out for any particularly bonkers driver. Lane markings were decorative rather than indicative. Despite their tiredness, they were energised by the prospect of seeing again the house—this building clad in buttermilk plaster in a state of picturesque decay—bought so precipitately and with so little deliberation. They were full of ideas. There was still much to do—it was a building site, albeit a picturesque one and with added sunshine.

They still felt the same thrill as they drew closer, but this time tinged with anxiety. The affair of the so-called 'neighbour.' What were they going to find?

It was crepuscular, almost dark, but still quite warm on this evening in late September when they finished climbing the winding mountain road and arrived at their driveway.

Sarah was thinking about the first time they had come to the house with the estate agent.

'We wondered where the hell we were going,' she told me. She added that this was also exactly what my late mother—the term 'outspoken' doesn't do her justice—had said on her first visit.

Luke turned into the driveway to park, pulling up smoothly to the gate, their gate. They were thankful to be here, but nervous. Home. *Cascina Cannella.* The gate was closed, but in the soft gloom of the night air they could see a note tacked on to the top spar.

'What's that?'

'No idea. Let's take a look?' Luke got out of the car to investigate. Sarah followed, tentative and slightly unnerved.

Chiudi il cancello (close the gate) was scrawled on the note, followed by another word they didn't recognise.

'Who do you think wrote it?' Sarah's face betrayed her concern. Luke put a hand on her shoulder.

'Don't worry. Let's just open up the house and worry about it in the morning. It's too late to do anything now. And I'm gasping for a cup of tea.' He smiled at her in the dusk and swung the gate open. Sarah tried to smile back, but she was disconcerted. She wondered what the other word meant, the one they didn't recognise. She wondered who had been prowling around their house. And she wondered why the writer thought he could tell them to close their *own* gate across their *own* driveway.

CHAPTER 5 *bis*

The importance of cake…

Sarah's summer fruitcake recipe
    180 gm caster sugar
    180 gm unsalted butter
    180 gm self-raising flour
    2 eggs
    Couple of squeezes of lemon juice
    Summer fruit

Put all ingredients into a bowl, except fruit, and mix up until well blended. Put mixture into a cake tin lined with greaseproof paper and sprinkled with sugar (this makes the bottom of the cake quite crispy and crunchy). Pile with a single layer of summer fruit, such as plums, apricots, figs or apples. Bake at 180 degrees C/gas mark 5 for about forty-five minutes.

CHAPTER 6
Choosing: Goodbye England

Piedmont
The present

It is a fine mid-autumn day, pleasantly warm. It is nearly lunchtime. We are sitting at the stone table in the garden, Sarah, Daisy and I, while Luke is devising something delicious in the kitchen. He keeps appearing at our table, bearing another dish of home grown vegetables, turned from earthy roots into oiled and herbed edible slices. This is Luke, a phantom, moving so swiftly and quietly it is a surprise to realise he is solid. If he needed the money, he could moonlight as a waiter, silent, effective, worth his weight in... sun dried tomatoes.

We are talking about that time, back at the tail-end of 2002, when Luke and Sarah made the choice, the life-changing choice—between staying in England, comfortable, prosperous, or Italy, uncomfortable, financially shaky.

Daisy is hungry and goads her son, shouts out:

'What's taking so long?'

Luke appears at the kitchen door in his flowery apron, wooden spoon in hand, frowning slightly.

'Won't be long, Mum. Hang on. I'm making broad bean salad, you love broad beans.'

'Third day in a row we've had broad beans. Haven't you got anything else?' Daisy is trying to wind him up, but he's not taking her on. She has an impish smile and looks years younger than her white hair suggests.

'You love broad beans, Mum,' he reiterates, as he disappears into the safety of the kitchen.

Daisy and I chuckle, but Sarah isn't listening. While we wait, pleasantly hungry, as garlicky, basil-laced scents drift around us, Sarah is gazing out over the valley, elbows resting on the table, pointed little chin held in her cupped hands.

When Luke returns with the broad bean salad—presenting it to his mother with a flourish and a smile—I ask how hard the decision was for him. He freely admits that when they bought the house in Italy, it was always his intention ultimately to live there full time.

Luke has been dreaming of living in Italy for most of his life. One time, when he was about eighteen and just finishing A levels, he applied for a work placement in Italy to learn the wine trade. He was put on the reserve list ('as always,' says Luke, shy about blowing his own trumpet). By the time he found out he had been accepted, he had decided to go to university to study food science.

'Someone obviously fell out and I got called up,' is how Luke explains it.

Sarah points out how lucky this was. If he'd gone to Italy, he wouldn't have gone to university—which is where they met. How different their lives would have been...

I am interested in finding out about what finally propelled Sarah to believe she could give up her English life. They bought the house in 1999. By 2003, they were going to Italy. They were only in their thirties, with no plan to retire to the sunshine.

'We didn't think about what we were taking on, how long it would take,' says Sarah, looking at me with that direct gaze, pondering the question.

'We had no idea really. We did literally follow a dream.'

Luke is urging us to eat, which isn't a difficult instruction. Before us, served in ceramic dishes, painted creamy yellow with splashes of clear green, echoing the colours of the food, we have courgette strips, sautéed in oil, sprinkled with parmesan; a broad bean salad, dressed in olive oil and balsamic vinegar (Daisy's favourite); buckwheat salad with tuna fish and sundried tomatoes; homemade bread (of course); and to round it all off, a selection of cheeses, accompanied by *cugna* (a kind of chutney).

Luke is a natural-born cook and is one of those people confident enough to adapt traditional recipes with success. He knows his ingredients—a lot of them he has grown or preserved—and is familiar with how flavours complement each other.

While we help ourselves to food, Sarah talks pensively, as if reliving the time she describes.

'At this stage, my job was going downhill. It wasn't as interesting as it used to be. I could have had a transfer to Croydon, but the thought of changing from commuting 100 miles every day to taking a train from rural Hampshire to Croydon every day, I couldn't do it any more.' Sarah groans, shrugs, shakes her head. The work, with its daily journey across Salisbury Plain, had become monotonous. Together, they had spent around thirteen years commuting to their respective jobs

'It just didn't feel like a life and there was something here pulling me.' Sarah hesitates, takes her elbows off the table, straightens her back, then seems to make a decision.

'This seemed more exciting, and I was quite happy to go because a lot of my friends were having a family… and we weren't. They had a new perspective on life. Everybody was changing. We needed to change.

'We were there, just there, stagnating…' Sarah adds.

There is a moment of silence.

There were other things, too, pressing on them, pushing them towards the decision. They yearned for a simpler life, but weren't sure how to create it, trapped in a financial comfort that didn't fulfil their longing for meaning. In England, everything was conspiring to persuade Sarah and Luke that moving to Italy was the right thing.

71

'I was being forced into a new and unlooked-for start anyway,' says Sarah.

'And I think another way this place pulled you is that you could see jobs being done, but they were being done badly, not properly,' Daisy chimes in, looking at her daughter-in-law knowingly. The two of them share a deep interest in the details of a house, in the materials used, the craftsmanship that goes into creating an interior—the right sheen of polish on the beam, the most sympathetic colour for a tile, the clean line of a wrought iron handle on a shutter.

'What about leaving everyone behind?' I ask. 'It must have been hard to leave your family, your friends?' I am imagining myself in the same situation. I lived for some years in North America, far from my family. I could only communicate through the (non-mobile) telephone, which was expensive and unsatisfactory, or by letter. Homesickness sometimes gripped me like a punch in the stomach. (In French, they say *'avoir le cafard'*—'having the cockroach,' for feeling blue or homesick; that sounds accurate).

'Yes, it was, it was very sad—and scary. Moving to a place where you know nobody and there is no one to ask advice from or share your thoughts with—even supposing you can speak the language. But it was exciting too. We dreamed about it for years. And...' Sarah stopped and looked at Luke. 'I think we were drawn to Italy because England was becoming too American—sorry, sorry,' she apologises, touches my arm in a conciliatory way. This is because of my penchant for American husbands (two, although not at the same time), my admiration for some aspects of US society and love of New York City, where I lived for four years. I let it pass, of course. A lot of English people feel the same way about Americans and are not afraid to let rip. My husband is used to it.

Lunch is nearly over, not much food left. Luke has served us with the tiny, pungent espressos.

'When I say, becoming too American, what I mean is all that "have a nice day" stuff, and the dirty brown water they call coffee, and the "love you's" all over the place.' Sarah can't stop herself.

'I think English people say "I love you" too.' We all laugh. Sarah sees she is going over the top, but by now, entrenched on her mountaintop, she feels vindicated.

'And all the consumerism, I mean it's disgusting.'

Luke and Sarah can't bear waste. Every bowl of washing up water is emptied onto the garden; leftover food is composted; vineyard cuttings are shredded and recycled. Everything feeds everything.

'It's the obscenity of too much choice, isn't it?' And of course, we all agree. And it occurs to me that what Sarah and Luke wish for is to recapture an older way of life. The fault lies not so much with England, or its submission to American fashions. Sarah and Luke are out of kilter with modern times.

When was the last time you had a conversation with a herbalist, for example?

Sarah has her own local herbalist. She walks through the door into the past. Wooden green drawers, each containing a different herb, line the walls of the shop from floor to ceiling. A tiny woman in a white coat presides behind the wooden counter.

'The room smells of herbs. I have to wait to be seen in a dimly-lit ornate waiting room, with a painted ceiling and framed photos of dried herbs covering the walls,' says Sarah, her voice full of delight.

When her turn comes, she receives advice on her diet, is given a cream for her skin, shampoo, and a mixture of herbs tailored especially for Sarah to make her tisane infusion. And all that for 33 euros and complete peace of mind.

Conversations these days in the local hardware shop can last a half hour at a time, as Sarah seeks the exact metal fixture or bit of garden equipment she needs.

The appeal of being much closer to the renovations was also powerful. Sarah realised she wanted not merely to oversee work on *Cascina Cannella*, but to get involved in the detailed refurbishment of the house and outbuildings. She was not content to relinquish control to someone else's imagination. And it was difficult to make decisions about the house when you weren't on the spot. In the two and half years she and Luke had spent on long distance building work, they had only seen the house nine times.

The obvious choice was to move properly to Italy and continue to work on renovating the Italian house.

'When you live in a house, it's difficult to decide where you want to put a light or even bigger things, like a bath, for example. But at a distance, plus using a foreign language to talk about things we knew nothing about in English, at times it seemed impossible,' Sarah says. And, as Daisy pointed out, Sarah is a stickler for painstaking workmanship.

At the beginning, she and Luke had much more to think about than where to put the bath. That kind of decision was the fun stuff, after all the grinding hard work of rebuilding.

The regular trips in those two or three years after the purchase were fun, invigorating, but quite disturbing. They found they missed the house more intensely each time they left. How was it faring, settling and shifting and creaking on its foundations, being buffeted by the extremes of weather, largely untended, uncared for, unkempt. After three years of sporadic building work on *Cascina Cannella* and spending hardly any money on the house in the UK, it became increasingly clear to Luke and Sarah that what they really wanted was to commit themselves entirely to the house—and indeed, to life—in Italy.

This was the house they wanted. This was the place they felt most at home.

*

Looking after a holiday house in a different country is not at all the same as casting off to another life. When Sarah and Luke bought their house, the challenges they faced in restoring the building and cultivating the land and the vineyard were great. No one was clamouring to take over the house that chose them. It had been empty for eight years, until they happened on it and fell happily prey to its decaying charm.

They were not yet forty years old when they made the decision to change their lives. They reasoned it would be easier at that age to meet people and make friends. Emotionally, you are not so young you are daunted by certain challenges nor so old you are stuck in your ways. In short, you can adapt. Luke managed to get a transfer with his current job, even though it meant losing certain advantages, including a pension.

This decision is not easy to make even when the finances might be secure and even when you are relatively young, but 'it felt right and exciting.' Sarah and Luke were neither too young to lack confidence, nor too old to be frightened of a potentially comfortless and tough existence.

On the financial front, they would have enough money to survive. However, the demands made by the complete abandonment of everything and everyone they knew fell mainly on Sarah. Not only would she have no job, and therefore, no readymade network of social and friendly contacts, but nor was she equipped with that Italian sensibility and connection to Italy by blood and history Luke could claim. She might yearn for a simpler, more traditional life and the advantages of self-sufficiency, but the old ways are not without drawbacks.

She would be on her own in a land where everyday sexism was disguised as excessively virile machismo, personified in the country's President at that time, Silvio Berlusconi. She would be seen as an adjunct to Luke, not a professional woman in her own right. And she would have to put aside all claims to status. She would be seen as simply a wife—and a foreigner.

It is all very well to visit a country, to adore its climate, food, culture and temperament. It is a different thing to learn how to live in a country—to negotiate its customs and understand its laws; interpret the attitudes of its citizens; carry out the everyday tasks that in your home country you can do without thinking, but in a less familiar country can seem unreasonably complicated.

Sarah and Luke were going to have to negotiate all of this and, moreover, would be obliged not only to behave like Italians, but more importantly, to think like Italians. If the project were to succeed, they would have to rely to an exceptional degree on their own strong relationship. Success would depend on them each taking responsibility for learning how to live the Italian way—not least, how to speak Italian effectively.

Most particularly, however, as they both acknowledge, the success or not of their venture would rest mainly on Sarah's slender shoulders.

After the years of leading a split existence, they made the decision. Everything around them was changing, yet at the same time, nothing was different. They felt their lives were not progressing; they were stagnating even while the society they lived in was no longer recognisable, nor as comfortable as it had been. Their friends were having families. Relationships were changing. They were ready for the next stage of their lives. *Cascina Cannella* called to them from its mountaintop. The house would be their destiny.

And then the death of their dearly-loved cat, Cinnamon, seemed like a signal. Take the plunge. Do it. Be courageous. Change your lives.

And they did. And they were. The effort was immense, the change profound.

CHAPTER 6 *bis*

Avoir le beurre et l'argent du beurre.

Indeed, looking after a holiday house in a different country is not at all the same as casting off to another life. It is more truly an attempt to have your cake and eat it. While I understand something of Sarah and Luke's experience, mine is much less dramatic. Even so, this split life, living in one country, trying to be part of another, is unsettling. Houses are like dogs. You can't ignore them. Without care and attention, they languish and die. Our house in France— a so-called *maison de vacances*—was anything but a holiday house. Whenever we went there, which was as often as work and school allowed, there were jobs waiting, some urgent, some not so urgent, but all essential.

Weather never ceases to torment. Buildings never cease to deteriorate. And grass never ceases to grow. Whenever we arrived in the early days, aside from the dead of winter, the grass would be up to our thighs and as tall as the children—much to their delight as we couldn't see them. And even when the children grew high enough to be seen, the grass was still waving at us, appearing to stretch as tall as can be, just to taunt.

The first summer, we installed the *fosse septique* (the beloved septic tank). A giant yellow digger forged a channel through the grass (take that, grass) and pipe with apertures laid to allow the sewage to drain into our garden from the main collecting tank. The children loved the giant yellow digger—they perched on the bedroom window ledge to watch—and we loved the fact that we now had a flushing toilet rather than a thunder box.

We tried to organise projects from a distance, but it was always difficult. You have to be there, on the spot, to make decisions, take measurements, be easy to contact.

Sometimes though, long-distance project management was a spectacularly smooth process, as in the case of the laying of the tiles across the entire ground floor. We had left the house emptied of all furniture. Beds, cupboards, the kitchen table, chairs, the stove, the dresser, anything that could be moved was moved outside into the garden, where it sat, draped in tarpaulins, for six weeks until we returned to the marvellous vision of a terracotta-tiled floorscape. It was magic. Where there was grey concrete, covered in damp bits of rug, now there was this gorgeous sunset orange floor beneath our feet. Hurray for wonderful French tilers. Hurray for trust in craftsmanship. Hurray for Anglo-French relations. Hurray for my mother, who paid for it. And then we had to heft the furniture back into the house...

Most often, it was all hands to the pump. Even the children, as they grew, had delegated tasks. Our daughter was given charge of the paintbrushes and the wood stain to paint the gate, along with a black plastic garbage bag with holes cut for head and arms. She has a tendency, even now, for covering herself in paint as well as her target. Our son likes dangerous tools, so of course, was never far from his grandfather and the circular power saw.

In current times, with half of Britain seeming to yearn for a return to pork pies and storage heaters, a '50s Britain of housewives and knowing your place and hating the French, the dream of owning a small plot in another country seems miraculous—or ridiculous.

In the nineties, however, such a dream was not regarded as treason, but rather as an act of grand imagination and good fortune. Buying a holiday house in a European country seemed within the grasp of many—much more so than in Britain, where buying a second home was largely the preserve of the rich. The opening of the channel tunnel in 1994 brought France and the rest of the continent closer. Leap on the train and thirty-five minutes later, there you are, on marvellous foreign soil, where everything smells different and you can slough off your regular identity and renew yourself in another fascinating culture.

Laying claim to a few hectares of European soil didn't require wealth so much as a taste for hard work, a positive attitude towards learning another language and a longing to experience a different way of life.

Nor did there appear to be the resentment of the foreigner coming in to buy up property and pushing out the local inhabitants. Our neighbours in Normandy, for example, assured us that no one wanted our house; it was far too primitive and rustic. It might have been left to slide gently into picturesque decay, were it not for that moment in November 1992, when we drove up the narrow farm lane and saw emerging from the damp misty air of an early Norman morning the solid stone walls and jaunty terracotta roof. It was exactly the house we had dreamed of.

Of course, it is not everyone's dream.

'What do you do there? Don't you get bored going back to the same place over and over again? Do you ever go anywhere else?' These are some of the questions I have heard over the years.

Looking after a second home is a commitment (we're not talking about second, third, fourth home owners as you may find in the various upper echelons of British society). Taking on a place that needs work to make it habitable means all your holidays will be spent tearing down old plaster, replacing it with new plaster; removing paint, then repainting; repairing or replacing shutters; woodworming, more woodworming, oh and then more woodworming; installing insulation; building staircases; persuading mice that you live there now and they have to move out... And I haven't even mentioned the plot of land choked with docks and stinging nettles and cow parsley and giant hogweed that is the 'garden.'

Of course this will not appeal to everyone.

Maybe what it offers, this toehold in another country, is a sense of belonging to a wider community than the one you grew up in and a broader understanding of the perspectives and views of others whose experience of life is different from yours. It is a looking outwards at the world, a welcoming in of the other rather than a rejection of it. Travelling to different countries offers a glimpse of the way people live, but from the outside. Living in another country, even if only part-time, is a privilege, an opportunity and a source of great joy.

*

Due ricette di Luke
(A couple of recipes from Luke)

Insalata di farro con tonno e pomodori secchi
Buckwheat salad with tuna and sun-dried tomatoes
     Cook the buckwheat in vegetable or chicken stock for 20 minutes, then sieve it. 'It's like cooking rice,' says Luke. After sieving, add lots of lemon, vinegar, oil, tuna fish, sun-dried tomatoes and fresh thyme. Season with salt and pepper.

Luke's cugna
This is a chutney made with everything that's in abundance in Piedmont in September: grapes boiled down, but not alcoholic, spices such as cinnamon and cloves, and different types of fruit, mainly pears, figs, peaches, chopped very fine. Bring the mixture to the boil and simmer it all day, stirring regularly until thick and glossy. And then you add the key ingredient, which is, of course... ground hazelnuts.

To go and buy something now seems quite strange to Sarah and Luke. They make all their own jam and preserves, not marmalade however. Oranges don't grow in Piedmont.

CHAPTER 7
Ciao Italia: The Arrival

'I've got something to confess.'

Luke was in the passenger seat of the truck. He kept looking straight ahead while Richard, his closest friend, parked the unwieldy vehicle at the top end of the driveway, in front of *Cascina Cannella*. This time, there was nothing barring their way. That was a relief. Luke hadn't even thought about it during the journey, but now he was here, he remembered a previous visit when he and Sarah had arrived at dusk and found that strange note pinned to the gate. Ah well, it would sort itself out.

'Uh huh,' Richard acknowledged distractedly. He was sturdily built, more of a Labrador in contrast to Luke, greyhound-lean. After twenty-one hours on the road, manhandling the 7.5 tonne truck, eyes stinging from the intense concentration, he was seriously ready to get into the house, stretch himself out on a flat surface and sleep. They had arrived, finally, at *Cascina Cannella,* full of cappuccino and bread and apricot jam. It was Luke's idea that they stop for breakfast in the nearby village rather than shopping for essentials right away, with the notion of having a nap before unloading the van and settling in. The final stretch of driving, manoeuvring the truck around the bends of the twisting mountain roads, was the last straw for Richard. He needed a place to rest.

'Yup. What's up?' Richard sat back, rubbing his eyes with the heels of his hands; his shoulders slumped under the thin cotton of his t-shirt, dark with sweat patches.

It was Easter-time, April 2003—the magical year. The big move. Goodbye England, *Ciao Italia.*

Sarah was not with them. The plan was for her to follow on by plane.

Luke ducked his head and put his hands up. Surrendering.

'I don't know where I put the keys,' he said, without looking at Richard's face.

There was silence.

'Weeeell… are you sure you brought them?' he asked eventually. Luke looked at him, finally. He wasn't sure. Richard's normally open face was a mask. He was working hard not to betray his feelings, which were a roiling mix of disbelief, irritation, disappointment and exhaustion. He had organised the packing. He was a good organiser. Luke and Sarah would not have been able to pack the truck without him. Richard oversaw the emptying of the house in England, dictated where everything should go in the truck, took care to make sure it was done properly. And he had enjoyed the journey, despite his initial nervousness. It was his first time driving abroad. The southern French city of Lyon had been particularly adventurous. A good sleep, stretched out at full length, muscles relaxed, eyes closed, a fluffy pillow for his head, would have been just right about now…

'I'm ninety per cent sure that the keys are in the truck,' Luke ventured, uncertainly. He had already ransacked the cab of the truck, turned out all available hiding spaces, felt through all the jacket pockets. But what if they weren't in the truck at all? It wasn't as if they had left a set of keys under the pot, or with a neighbour. (Luke grimaced inadvertently—imagine relying on the man next door, he would probably just use them to snoop.)

At least it wasn't raining, Luke thought, as they opened the back doors of the truck and surveyed the contents, rammed into every available space. He was only wearing cotton shorts, even though when they set off—when was that? it felt like days—the Hampshire drizzle had lowered the air temperature and it was pretty chilly.

He started taking things out of the truck and piling them onto the driveway. It was still quite early in the day, but warm already in this month of April. Those twenty-one hours on the road were taking their toll on him too, even though with the passing of each hour, he had been aware of his excitement mounting, for he was being carried nearer to the start of this new reality, this new life.

The unloading on to the road, which ran alongside the high, grey wall of the neighbouring house, did not go unnoticed. There was a row of windows situated a good two and a half metres up the wall, plenty of scope for surveying the driveway.

'Just so long as we find the keys,' Luke was thinking, as they got closer and closer to the back of the van. Where could he have stowed them. There had to be an obvious answer. Sarah would know. Sarah knew everything. But there was no way of getting in touch with her, no phone. Oh hell.

'If we can't find the keys we'll just have to break in,' said Richard, thrusting his shoulders back and his chest out. 'Maybe there's a window open. Or we can kick a door in.'

Luke's heart didn't just sink, it lurched against his ribs, did a full somersault and then plummeted to the bottom of his stomach. It would not be at all easy to break in. They had already installed solid beech doors, equipped with bolts. And the windows? He could picture them taking an axe or a chisel or a hammer (whatever he and Richard managed to lay their hands on), smashing the freshly installed glass panes, splitting the wood of the original frames into splinters, no use even for kindling. Sarah would be beside herself.

And then, suddenly, he saw them. The keys. Saw them in his mind's eye, nestling in his sock drawer, which was in the old pine chest of drawers with the brass handles, one of the first pieces of furniture they had loaded, oh so many hours ago, and was, therefore, at the very back of the van…

It wasn't only the failure to safeguard the keys that was bothering him. Something else was gnawing at his brain. What was it?—ah yes, that weird handshake. He had come over to *Cascina Cannella* a few months ago in January. It was absolutely freezing, snow lying thickly everywhere. The moisture in your nostrils froze so that when you breathed in, they stuck together. His brother Michael had accompanied him. The problem was a water pipe that had risen slightly out of the ground and was now standing proud and exposed to the freezing air, with the result that the water was also freezing. The cause lay with the house next door. Luke and Michael were compelled to talk to the 'neighbour,' who was in fact not so much a neighbour as a self-appointed guardian of the empty house. It had still not been sold, but *Signor* X had apparently decided to move in anyway, although he occupied the house only during the day. At a certain time each evening, he left to go… where? Luke had no idea and didn't care. This neighbour was already occupying too much of the space in Luke's head.

They managed to sort out the problem reasonably. Luke tried to bid the neighbour a polite farewell. It was in all their interests. As Luke extended his hand, you could see the neighbour struggling to reciprocate, as if something had hold of his elbow and was preventing full extension of the arm. He could hardly bring himself to offer his own hand, almost as if it were deformed or was in fact a hook. ('By God, Mum,' Michael told Daisy later, 'they've got some trouble there.')

Luke looked around him as they continued unloading the contents of his and Sarah's old life from the back of this ordinary white van. Was he watching this, the neighbour with the most reluctant handshake in Piedmont? Luke glanced up involuntarily at the immense concrete-clad wall that reared above the side of the driveway, casting them into shadow on this bright sunlit day. It made him think of a castle in a fairy tale, but a castle that sheltered an ogre rather than a princess.

*

Sarah was glad Richard was driving. Before the moving day —she could hardly believe how quickly that day dawned once they had made the decision—she worried about having to drive the truck. She and Luke, equal partners in most things, always shared the driving on their regular trips to Italy (even though she was a nervous driver), but she didn't want to admit to Luke how much she did *not* want to share the driving when they moved all their belongings to Italy. Sarah was always a determined person, keen to set goals for herself. She was unhappy about her fear. Luke's older brother, Michael, offered to drive, but Sarah did not trust him. The last time they had been on a road trip with Michael, they got lost in the first five minutes. Besides, driving an Alfa Romeo is not the same as driving a big van. (Luke and Michael remain loyal to all things Italian, including cars, of course.)

When Richard, with his taste for adventure, offered to help, Sarah felt enormous relief flood through her, out of all proportion to her fear of driving.

Dismantling their home proved a challenge. They had lived in the house in Hampshire for thirteen years. You accumulate a lot of stuff in that time. It took seven days to pack the entire house into carefully labelled boxes. There was no knowing how long everything would have to stay in those boxes. None of the rooms in the Italian house were remotely ready to take all the furniture. It was still an old derelict house, even if partially restored. They had the conveniences—power, water—but nothing was in any kind of decorative order and certainly not in any state to be furnished, beyond what was necessary.

Friends helped them pack the truck. They drank their coffee sitting on garden furniture at the side of the road. Then they set off, Luke at the wheel for the first leg of the journey. While the small group of friends waved and whooped, Sarah stood apart from them, clutching her coffee cup tightly with both hands, watching as the truck drew further and further away from her and from their house, their life.

*

And now she was standing in the gravelly yard outside the kitchen of the Italian house, again clutching a coffee cup, again waving goodbye to Luke and Richard, but this time, she had no friends to turn back to. She was alone.

This was how they had planned it. Luke would return to Piedmont once he and Richard had returned the van to the Hampshire rental place. He would drive the car back across the length of France to reach *Cascina Cannella*, which presumably would not take as long as the drive to the UK in the truck. Even so, however quickly he drove (and Luke liked driving fast), the journey back to Italy was still going to take eleven to thirteen hours. Sarah calculated that she was contemplating at least three days by herself.

When she arrived, not quite believing that here she was, finally, after all the planning, dreaming, packing, she found Luke and Richard well ensconced. The elusive keys had been found—indeed, they were in the sock drawer (of course), the windows were intact (Richard did not have to bash them in, Luke was spared having to explain the destruction to Sarah), it was possible to make a decent cup of coffee. However, the logical plan that they had made— for Luke and Richard to return the van, then for Luke to come back by car—seemed completely illogical, for she would be all alone. Why had that not occurred to her? Her career up until this point had been devoted to forethought and planning.

Sarah did not want to be left alone, but nor did she want to admit that she did not want to be alone. Anyway, all the doors and windows could be locked; the house could be made secure. It was not like the early days, when there was no glass in the windows. Sarah thought about the time her sister stayed with her a couple of summers ago, when the two of them had barricaded themselves into the house and barely slept. It was different now.

The trouble was, it didn't *feel* different. The house was open on all sides. There were no fences, no gates. Growth and vegetation, yes, but no real physical barriers. Defenceless.

Sarah stood a long time, still clutching her coffee cup. She walked away from the house towards the vineyard and stood looking out over the valley.

'What have I done?'

She turned back to the house, intending to pour another cup of coffee and shake off this sudden sense of desolation. She *was* all alone here. And then she had the odd sensation that she was not as alone as she thought, that someone, something, was watching. She looked over her left shoulder, towards the slope where the vineyard grew. Nothing. Silence. Barely even a breeze ruffling the leaves. She continued briskly towards the kitchen, unnerved.

Sarah all alone

There was a knock on the door. Darkness had already fallen. The moon was wreathed in mist. Sarah jumped, her heart pounding uncomfortably against her chest; she found it difficult to swallow. It was only about seven o'clock in the evening, but with Luke still not back from England, she had already made her rounds of the doors and windows, locking and securing them before darkness descended. Who on earth could it be? She knew hardly anyone. She leaned against the door, as if barricading it. This was the first time that she had been completely by herself in the house since they bought it. She could fill her day with activities, but the night lent itself to little but sleep. There were few diversions—she couldn't get a clear radio signal for English language radio, they hadn't got a television. Reading at night required resilience, a determined ignoring of unidentifiable sounds as the house settled and creaked, still unused to its new inhabitant.

'*Signora Rinaldi, tutto bene? Hai bisogno di qualcosa?*

Oh relief. It was *Signor* Rossi, 'the man in the vineyard.' He had come to see if she needed anything.

Sarah struggled to get out a sentence of reassurance in her beginner's Italian. She still didn't open the door, but he seemed satisfied and bade her '*Buonanotte.*'

Signor Rossi and his tiny, agile wife Sofia (she could climb a tree like a monkey, Sarah said) took Sarah and Luke under their wing soon after they first bought the house. Weather-beaten Signor Rossi, continually ruddy-skinned, whatever the season, was a local *contadino*, a farmer born and bred in Piedmont.

He and Sofia lived just a couple of kilometres up the hillside. Each time Sarah and Luke arrived for their holiday at *Cascina Cannella*, they would be greeted with a beautiful basket of vegetables, nuts, fruit and eggs, left for them in their courtyard.

The Rossis tended Sarah and Luke's small vineyard (about 0.2 of a hectare), had done so for years, and wanted to continue, which was convenient for everyone. It was going to take some time before they would be able to get their heads round the responsibilities of running a vineyard, however small. And meantime, it gave them some income. The Rossis paid them a token rent and sold the grapes to a wine making co-operative.

Once *Signor* Rossi had departed, Sarah continued with her evening, eating something (what? she barely knew, she had been so unnerved by the knocking, however kindly meant), passing the time somehow before a not-too-early bedtime, so that she could be sure of sleeping. In fact, she slept badly. These few days before she could expect Luke to return felt like a week. It's not as if she could call him. She had no phone, no car and nobody nearby to call on...

*

He just seemed to materialise out of nowhere. One moment, Sarah was alone. The next moment, she wasn't.

This morning, as usual, she had stepped out of the kitchen onto the patch of scrub outside the back door (the courtyard, she called it to herself, liking the grandeur, wanting to give the house its dignity) with her small cup of dark and tangy espresso—they might not have a proper kitchen, but the coffee was magnificent—when she realised she wasn't alone. There was a figure, a short stocky man, with a bristly scalp, just over to her left beyond the yard's boundary. She turned her head abruptly to look properly, but the figure had disappeared. Ah, the elusive, yet ever present neighbour.

'Weird,' she thought. Should she seek him out?

The house next door was still not sold, officially, but they were by now well acquainted with their neighbour. There was the business with the overhanging roof—when was that? Back in 2000 when they had that phone call from *Signor* Pozzi? And then there was the note he left on their gate one time, and then the continuing silliness over the driveway, their driveway. At least, that's what they thought it was, just silliness. And other things, things Sarah could not quite define: a shadowy presence, a continual observing, a feeling of someone there and yet not there. She hadn't got a good look at him. In the few dealings they had with him, Luke took the lead because of his superior language ability. And Sarah had been quite happy to leave those awkward interactions to Luke. In her head, she imagined him as John Wayne, the old Hollywood actor, famous in the mid-twentieth century, who walked with legs slightly bowed as if he'd just got off his horse, a gruff, unfriendly, scowling man always on the lookout for his enemy.

John Wayne only appeared during the daylight hours. Sarah was always relieved at the end of the day, because she knew he didn't live in the house next door. She knew that by a certain time of day he would go home, wherever home was. She had become aware of his routine. He would arrive at a certain time in the morning, leave at a particular time in the evening. That was the moment she felt able to breathe again properly. All day long, she had the sensation of having to hold her breath, or to breathe lightly, to allow her ears to pick up any movement, any slight rustling, any sound she could not immediately recognise, locate and name.

*

Luke turned off the engine of the hot, dusty and tired Alfa Romeo, put on the handbrake and took a deep breath. He was exhausted. He had driven for something like thirteen hours straight at speeds of barely less than ninety miles an hour and his head spun. He just wanted to get out of the car, stretch his legs and take in this moment. He had arrived in his new life. Finally. After all the work, the planning, the anguish of leaving. As he stood beside the Alfa, not quite ready to let go of this moment, a presence, a very solid human presence smelling of onions, made itself felt at his shoulder.

'*Sposta la macchina,*' commanded the stocky man, pointing at Luke's car and gesturing for him to take it away.

Luke recognised him as the neighbour/self-appointed guardian who was occupying the house next door —'handshake man' himself.

He didn't want to argue.

'*Sono stanco. Lasciarmi in pace.*'

Luke just wanted the angry man buzzing round him to go away and leave him in peace. He was too tired to be polite. This was, after all, his driveway, whatever the angry man believed. He could see nothing wrong with leaving his car there.

'*Che problema c'e?*'

Luke turned to the car, locked it, turned his back on buzzing handshake man and walked towards the house, towards Sarah and home.

*

They were here, at last, after all the dreaming, the planning, the organising, then the acts of relinquishing, of saying goodbye, of parting... *Cascina Cannella* was their home. There would be no going back.

Luke was damned if he was going to let the neighbour rain on their parade, on their dream. Neither he nor Sarah knew what lay behind his hostility, but there had to be a solution to this falling out. Sarah always felt better when she could devise a means of fixing a situation.

They would have to make an effort to get to know the neighbour, Sarah decided, try to start their relationship again, after the scratchy confrontations that had so far occurred. That would be the best thing, the normal, courteous thing. It might help to banish this slight sense of... what? Menace? So far, the only other people Sarah had any social contact with in the neighbourhood were the Rossis. That was it. Nobody else.

And the Rossis were perfectly pleasant, indeed welcoming. Their regular baskets of edible greetings, laid at Sarah and Luke's back door, through the years of to-ing and fro-ing, allayed all of Sarah's fears about being shunned as an outsider. (Luke was never assailed by such fears. Living as an Italian came naturally to him.)

The solution was to be a gift of hazelnut shortbread biscuits, a nice fusion of cultures, Scottish shortbread,

Piemontese hazelnuts, signifying a willingness to get along. Sarah wrapped it in what she considered to be an attractive way.

She was pleased with herself. Her package of cookies was delightful. It looked like she had gone to a lot of trouble, all frills and furbelows. She and Luke picked a day of fine spring weather to make their offering. The valley was awash with the fresh greens of the vineyards and the more substantial, darker greens of the trees. On their land —you couldn't really call it a garden yet, it was a tangle of old tomato and zucchini plants—the blues and pinks and purples of the rosemary and thyme broke up the green rhythms. Luke was home for a few days. They had much work to do on the house, as ever, but they were relaxed, ready to face gruff John Wayne with the reluctant handshake.

They went next door—which sounds so easy, so innocuous. But it wasn't like knocking on the front door, aglow with stained glass inserts, of a pretty semi-detached cottage in Hampshire. They had to negotiate the knotty vegetation and iron railings of the neighbour's 'compound' to approach the entrance, and even then, a simple knock wasn't going to do it. They had to rap several times with fists on the heavy beechwood door.

The neighbour's wife opened for them. Her plump figure was clothed in pink fluffy top and white trousers. She looked clean and laundered, thought Sarah as she shook the *Signora's* manicured hand, the nails a shiny matching pink. Such a contrast to Sarah, with her customary cottons— today, a pair of drawstring pull-on trousers and a linen tunic—and nails lined with dirt from gardening. *Signora X* did not look like the other country people around here. Nor did she smell like them. What was that perfume? Sarah had no idea. Perfume wasn't her style. The scent was heavy, the kind a great blowsy peony should have. Was there an undertone of mustiness?

'Ah Signor, Signora, per favore entrate.'

Sarah waited for Luke to step over the threshold, quite shy. Her lack of decent Italian made her feel helpless. She put a hand on his back to encourage him to go in ahead of her. He was wearing his smart blue linen shirt with the faint stripe running through it, she noticed. He was making more of an effort. Perhaps she should have dressed up a bit. Oh dear, too late. At least she had brushed her hair and put on some lipstick.

Signora X ushered them in. Then *Signor X* emerged to take his place beside his wife. He was not some fearsomely built sinister figure à la Godfather but a short, stocky man in his sixties with a greyish bristle covering his head. He had the curiously bulky upper body paired with the short legs, held deliberately wide, that are sometimes the hallmark of the self-consciously small man.

After exchanging some remarks—conversation would be too grand a word for what passed between them—Sarah proffered the package to *Signora X* who took it with a slight look of puzzlement. This was nothing compared with the look on *Signor X's* face. It was thunderous. He was staring at the package, gloriously wrapped in purple tissue paper and bound with black ribbon. Sarah was not only disappointed, but baffled at his reaction.

Sarah subsequently found out from her Italian teacher that Italians could be superstitious and that one of the superstitions concerns the meaning of colours. The deep purple of the tissue paper brings bad luck. The glossy black of the ribbon signifies death...

'How was I to know?' Sarah asked herself. But this became a source of guilt. Why hadn't she thought to do some research into local customs, asked someone the best way to make friends with neighbours in rural Piedmont? There was no pervasive internet, of course. She would have had to make the effort to visit the library, find the right book, translate the relevant passage. This was not the kind of mistake Sarah would have made in her previous efficient and well-managed life. But this life was nothing like that one. The rules had changed.

CHAPTER 7 *bis*

When you give me oysters, I clam up…

Negotiating local ways of behaving, local customs, local manners in a foreign country is not simple. Fear of causing offence means you often do. You can't avoid it. Leaving the shop without a courteous '*Au revoir, messieurs dames*' in France is rude. Not shaking hands on meeting your neighbour, an acquaintance, a visitor, is rude. Rejecting your neighbour's bag of oysters offered to you when you've just moved in is rude. You don't mean to be rude; you just don't know the intentions or the protocols. And especially if you are British, you fear being embarrassed, so you bluster and snort out phrases and are generally offensive, particularly when being offered oysters, because oysters are not the same as a cup of tea.

This is what our neighbour offered us in the early days of our French life and we were so taken aback we rejected them '*Non, merci.*' I then spent a whole afternoon pondering the significance of the oysters and realised it was a friendly and generous gift. I had to rectify our mistake. It was a rainy summer's day, not untypical of *Basse Normandie*, so I shrugged on a waterproof jacket over my shorts and t-shirt, dragged on the wellington boots and ventured next door, leaving my mother and children to fend for themselves with crayons at the kitchen table. I passed the proud (but tied up) Whisky, the neighbour's small, observant dog, coated with tufts of chestnut fur, who was surveying the landscape from the top of his kennel, and approached the neighbour's door, nervous. It opened before I had time to knock. *Monsieur* Fournier, the neighbour, with his red stubbly cheeks and cigarette in his mouth, was standing there, looking stern, or so I thought. The complicated notions in my brain about the nuances of refusing oysters because I didn't recognise how generous a gift they were and because I didn't know if he was selling them or what was going on, all had to be reduced to clear sentences. It was a struggle. What I had understood to be a severe expression on M. Fournier's face was, in fact, horror at having to deal not only with a woman, but with a foreign woman. He was extremely shy.

I took the oysters home, we shucked them in the garden, dressed them with lemon juice and pepper, and slid them down our throats, as if tasting the sea, and we toasted M. Fournier and our fantastic luck at being allowed to be here in this fantastic place.

CHAPTER 8
Sarah through the looking glass

Piedmont, summer 2003

As months passed, they settled into their lives. Sarah was becoming more used to the idea of Italy. She loved standing with her coffee in the 'courtyard' outside the back door. April passed, then May. The seasons were so much more extreme than at home in England. (At home? England was no longer home.) Sarah often thought about her Hampshire garden that she had nurtured through the early years of her marriage to Luke. Thought of snowdrops in late winter, the lawn covered in dewy spider webs in the chilly early morning mist. Thought of the tender pale green leaves of the forsythia uncurling to replace the dying yellow flowers, the first to arrive. Thought of her happy surprise as the tulips poked their heads through the soil in their pots, always earlier than she remembered.

Gazing over this valley with its shifting colours—bright emerald greens of the nut and fruit trees, purple-toned cypresses, splashes of crimson and yellow roses, threaded through the vines—Sarah again felt joy. She was overcome with the exhilaration of when she and Luke had first encountered this place, this house, this *territory*. She was more able now to withstand the night-time fears when Luke was away.

Their neighbours, the Rossis, continued to watch over them. The baskets of produce continued to turn up, even though Sarah and Luke were now full-time residents, no longer holiday visitors. That first year, *Signor* Rossi was keen to know if they were going to make *un orto*, a vegetable plot, of their own. When they said yes, he turned up the very next day, equipped with his tractor, and created a brand new *orto* for them. He then proceeded to plan what vegetables would grow, bought the seeds and planted them too at the appropriate time, the time of the full moon.

Signor Rossi's neighbourliness didn't stop there. He came around every week, checking on the progress, giving advice, watering and hoeing. Ever the pessimist, never content with conditions as they were, he complained it was too hot, too cold, too wet.

Luke's job took him away frequently. He was often on the road for three or four days. Sarah was used to this. When they lived in the UK, they both had jobs that involved travelling. The difference in Italy was that Sarah no longer travelled. She was the point of return, the keeper of the house. She didn't want to be the kind of person that wishes time away, but she couldn't help it. She was fiendishly busy, but time remained fiendishly slow when Luke was gone, flowing on by in the pastoral rhythm of the surrounding countryside, neither hurrying obligingly, nor becoming treacly and sluggish, just ticking gently while Sarah set to with her tools and cleaning materials, so busy, so efficient, so lonely.

Being busy, staying busy, was essential to Sarah's wellbeing at that time.

*

'Every day I was busy.'

'You started on the renovations right away?'

'Yes.'

'You kept yourself really busy?'

'Yes.'

I can tell my questions are starting to irritate Sarah. Her voice has a slight edge. Normally softly-spoken, at least speaking English, Sarah shows her feelings not so much through a change in volume but in the length of sentences. She becomes more clipped.

It is a mild evening in mid-October. There is a slight breeze outside, whispering across the darkening valley. Still no rain. The land is longing for it, after the enormously hot summer of 2017. We are eating one of Luke's wonderful meals (that he seems to create so effortlessly) in the 'dining room.' This is quite a grand room, longer than it is wide, standing in the location of the former hayloft, at right angles to the main house. It is full of the furniture Sarah has built out of discarded wooden doors and window frames and rusted metal tools. When you enter through the double doors, stepping in from the stone courtyard, you see yourself in a vast gilt-framed mirror that glows golden in the candle light against the honey-coloured stone walls. It feels as if you are entering a mediaeval banqueting room. The long table (made from an old pine door unearthed somewhere by Sarah) is laid with a wax tablecloth and linen place mats. In the centre are giant pinecones so big you think they must have been carved out of wood. Each object has a purpose, the bowl of fruit, the basket of bread, and yet each brings with it a splash of beauty. Some of the pine panels incorporated into the two dressers Sarah has created still bear scrapings of the original turquoise green paint. There is a dash of crimson somewhere—a picture? a ceramic bowl? a minstrel's doublet? a wall-hanging? Well, almost. It is a place out of time.

I have the feeling Sarah is so settled now, so content, that to bring back the fears of the early days is a struggle. She prefers not to remember. But I persist, because I am obtuse sometimes and imagine I am being sensitive.

'What was busying you at that point? You didn't have a job.'

'I worked on the kitchen.'

'You kept yourself really busy? You started on the renovations right away? I'm trying to get into your head.' I laugh lightly, but the tension remains.

'Every day I was busy.'

'You just got on with it. Anything you could do without a builder, you did?'

Finally, Sarah relents, starts to open. 'Yes. I had to get the kitchen decorating done before the kitchen was installed. So I sanded all the beams, sculpted all the beams, polished all the beams, sealed the ceiling, made sure the dust wasn't coming down, painted all the walls, filled in all the cracks, basically prepared everything for when the kitchen was arriving. Took about six weeks.'

I change the subject slightly. How were they making meals at this point? What parts of the kitchen were functioning?

'It was primitive,' says Sarah. 'Basically, we had a cooker, just for heating things. When we arrived—I mean to live here—the bathrooms were installed. The kitchen had plumbing to the sink but nothing else. The heating was in. But… everywhere needed decorating. It was horrible, disgusting. Very dirty. So you bring what you've got in England, so clean, to a very dirty environment.' She seems to be reliving the early days now, but not the joy of them, more their harshness and discomfort.

Then, as we settle for another delicious course from Luke's kitchen—figs in red wine syrup with the homemade ice cream (of course), flavoured with *pasta di nocciola* (hazelnut paste, not homemade—shocking—but supplied by a local producer who lives five minutes' drive away), Sarah's memories take flight.

'I came here. I spent six weeks on the kitchen. Then I moved to another room, six weeks. Each room took roughly about six weeks. It wasn't at all what the builders said: *'metti un po di vernice bianca*—put on a bit of white paint.' I was so tired at the end of the day. In fact, I remember getting so tired one day that after I had my shower, sitting on the front doorstep, I drank a very bad bottle of red wine. (Sarah rarely drinks more than a glass or two.) I had a really bad headache the next day and I remember thinking *"What am I doing here?"* At this point Sarah's voice rises, after the almost deadpan account. 'It did feel very odd...' she tails off.

'You had no mobiles. You couldn't just call Luke and say, "I've had a crap day,"' I prod gently.

'No. And also we didn't really have the internet set up either, so we didn't have emails. That was a big novelty when we got the emails.' Sarah's English is becoming slightly foreign, as if she is returning from the past to her everyday Italian life and thinking in the language that she more naturally uses now.

*

When she wasn't working on the house, Sarah was roaming the streets looking for company.

After the hazelnut biscuit disaster, Sarah was even more determined to conquer the Italian language. She was done with half measures. If she had been able to express herself more clearly, maybe their relationship with the neighbour would not have deteriorated so.

In the early days, Sarah felt she was falling, falling but never reaching solid ground.

'Anyone I heard speaking English in the street, I would stop them, which is bizarre, stupid,' she says, her eyes wide and serious. We all make a sort of grunting sound, me, Daisy and Luke, which is neither laughter nor surprise, but recognition—how does it feel not to be able to speak, not to be able to make yourself understood, not to make human connections? A picture pops into my mind of Sarah, a small English woman in her thirties, attractive, blonde, roaming around the hot, intimidating streets of the local town, accosting people at random. Was this wise?

Sarah depended on the kindness of strangers. She looked at the adverts wherever they were displayed—local shops, public places, newspapers. Once, Sarah found an advert for someone to teach English. Without any real thought of what it would mean to teach English to a person, how you would go about it, she rang up because she thought, 'Oh they can speak English.' And she was able to make friends with the parent of a student. It was an opening, albeit brief.

'If you don't know anybody and you can't speak the language, how are you going to meet anybody? Everybody needs somebody…' Sarah trails off with what sound like the lyrics of some half-remembered song. But then she is back into her stride again.

'Like in supermarkets, if I heard someone speaking English, I would talk to them.'

The supermarket turned out to be a good place to run into English speakers. A spot of communication over the zucchini.

'Fair enough. A small town. I can see that,' I encourage her. Sarah doesn't need much encouragement. You can tell she is transported to those early days when she and Luke had first moved to Piedmont for good and she could hardly tell who she was any more. Life had been turned upside down and Sarah had never imagined how differently she would feel now that the Italian house was home and not some place she could leave after a few weeks.

'Exactly,' she continues, 'I'd think perhaps they might be in the same situation, they might want to meet somebody. There's a lady I know over there.' Sarah points vaguely towards the doorway of the dining room, open to the dark valley and the sprinkled stars, 'that I met in the town hall. I said, "I've just bought a house in Italy." I was shy before coming here. I would never have gone up to anybody, but it's a need, isn't it? Otherwise, well, nobody was going to come and knock on *my* door, were they?'

Sarah looks at us expectantly, her eyes bright. She has no idea how nuts she sounds. We all rally round, with murmurs of how humans are sociable, have a need to communicate and so on. 'Well, we are a social animal,' Daisy chirps up.

103

Sarah continues blithely, 'and also you've got to be part of society. You've got to be you. If you can't communicate with somebody, nobody knows who you are.'

In life before Italy, Sarah's job was to manage the importing of food products from factories abroad into the UK. She was responsible on the technical side, for packaging and quality, and responsible for the private label (non-supermarket) customers bringing their products from abroad. This involved travelling to France, Germany, Switzerland, Spain—all over Europe—by car and usually alone.

'I'm not a very good driver and I'm quite a timid person,' Sarah tells us.

('Timid' or 'shy' are not the first adjectives that spring to mind to describe Sarah. In the old days, before Italy, she seemed to the rest of the family formidable. There were clues to her inner shyness, but these were not easy to spot. When she was surrounded by our family, with Daisy and her sisters Violet, my late mother, and May, the oldest of the triumvirate, boisterously at the controls, she would withdraw slightly so that her shyness appeared to be aloofness. In truth, they were a little frightened by Sarah and her self-containment. The three sisters, led by my mother, formed an opinionated trio. At Sarah and Luke's wedding party, Violet heckled her nephew Luke throughout his speech so that he barely made it to the end. She didn't dare heckle Sarah. Daisy calls her, with admiration, 'the lady Sarah.' This has nothing to do with class and everything to do with character.)

'I travelled all over the place at a time when there were no mobile phones. I was travelling all over these countries, in the middle of nowhere, crossing my fingers that the car wouldn't break down,' says Sarah. 'I suppose it was a big fear to come here. But I wanted to do it. I've always said if you hate to do something, you should do it. You should get over that fear.'

I was struck by this remark. Moving to Italy appears a beautiful dream. Many are fascinated by the notion of being able to voluntarily abandon their everyday lives and remake themselves elsewhere. And if that 'elsewhere' is the arresting landscape of rural Piedmont, with its terraced vineyards and shady hazelnut groves, it is easy to ignore the difficulties and dwell only on the beauty. Yes Sarah wanted to make her life with Luke in Italy, but she was also very fearful. It was something she had not admitted openly.

'Did you give yourselves a time limit?' I am back to the interrogation.

'No. We'd sold everything in England,' Sarah says, not understanding my point.

'You might have kept a flat there, or something?' I persist.

'I'm not sure how much we thought, to be honest.' Sarah frowns.

'Just got on and did it really,' Luke adds.

He is busy clearing after dinner, going to and from the kitchen across the courtyard carrying table debris. Luke always seems occupied, but unobtrusive, like the best waiters. You hardly notice what he's doing, but your plate is suddenly furnished with a plump slab of lasagne and your glass refilled. The rest of us are sitting around the table, happily full of Luke's fine food, faces lit only by candlelight and a couple of wall lights, which Sarah has made out of roof tiles. Dinner is over, but Daisy and I are finishing our glasses of rich red Barbera (always the ones whose glasses are never empty).

'Did you check in with Sarah when you were travelling all over Italy and the rest of Europe for work? Did you have a mobile phone by then?' I ask Luke as he takes a momentary break from clearing the table, and sits—to listen, to savour a drop more of the wine. He sticks his nose in the glass to make the most of the late summer aroma of black cherries. The candles have burned low, we have only a little wine left in our glasses and it is getting late.

'Probably, by 2003,' Luke says, looking at Sarah.

'No, you didn't check in,' she says.

'I suppose people used to do that though, didn't they? There would be great absences and then, all of a sudden, there you were, home.' I laugh. (I remember this vividly from my time as a student in France. I communicated with my family and friends mainly by telegram and letter, so that you might arrive virtually at the same time as your message. Very Henry James. The telephone system was expensive and involved complicated visits to the *bureau de poste* (post office) where you booked your call at the counter and bought the *jetons*—tokens—you pushed into the telephone box before you could speak. Once the person at the counter had placed the call, you then entered a private cabin to speak, remembering to push in the *jetons*.)

'The good old days,' says Luke, with a smile. We all laugh.

'But you didn't think, "Is she going to be okay?" You just assumed she would be?'

There is a long silence, then Sarah laughs. 'That's a good question.'

After a while, Luke responds, 'I just don't remember.'

I push on. 'I'm just curious—not because she's a woman or anything like that, but because she was a person on her own?'

'Of course I was worried about her, but I suppose I trusted that she would get on with things. But I knew that if she wasn't happy, then this adventure wouldn't work.'

Sarah recalls when they first arrived, after quitting England for good. 'I remember thinking what a beautiful place, and I'm really happy to be here, but what have I left? All my friends, all those people I've gathered over the years, and I've left my family behind. I've left everybody behind. And I can't speak anything; I can't communicate with anybody. I'm not a professional person any more, just Luke's wife.'

*

When she first moved to Italy, Sarah was particularly anguished about lacking enough language to express herself. Her GCSE in Italian had ill equipped her to speak in anything other than transactional phrases. She could manage to shop for groceries, make herself understood in the *panetteria* (bakery) and ask directions. Beyond that, she was imprisoned in her English high castle, desperate to say more than '*200 grammi di parmigiano per favore*' (200gm of Parmesan cheese please), struggling to make herself visible.

These days, her English is peppered with Italian words —they come to her more easily than the English equivalents. But at the beginning, she would repeatedly ask herself questions, carry on an inner dialogue: *What am I going to do? I can't live like this. I've got to learn the language, because if I can't speak the language, nobody will know who I am. I can talk about, yes, the weather's lovely, but they will never know who I really am.*

You might almost call this an existential crisis. Sarah was questioning her authenticity.

*

When Sarah was roaming the streets of her local town, or neighbouring villages, and ensnaring English speakers in haphazard conversations, this was odd behaviour not just by other people's standards, but also by her own. It's a sign of that desperate need for human conversation. She admits that it is a bit strange going up and talking to someone —'that's probably why I didn't meet many people that way'—but the upside was that she overcame some of her shyness and did meet a range of people from diverse backgrounds, different countries, who had made their homes in Piedmont. She reasoned that someone might be in the same situation as her, that they might want to meet somebody too. She picked up a range of friendships in this random way, although most did not last. They were a step towards belonging, a stopgap.

From the start, she and Luke were very concerned to make the Italian way of life theirs. Sarah was determined not to fall into the expatriate trap. She did not want to create a little England in Italy. 'I met English people here because their husband had got a job—they were having tea parties and things like that. But that's not why I'm here, I don't want to be part of an English colony.'

Not all of the 'foreigner-friendships' faded, however, as they became more integrated into Italian ways. Sarah made the happy acquaintance of an older couple, two American women who had lived in Piedmont most of their adult lives. The two women and Sarah developed a satisfying bond. Sarah was particularly fond of Leah: small, sturdy and practical. They shared a taste for getting things done. Bobbie, on the other hand, with her grey curls that shouted 'you are welcome, I am friendly' was most at home in the kitchen and garden. The pair took Sarah under their wing. They lived in a vast farmhouse, which sprawled over a hill that sloped down to a river, glimpsed through a sprinkling of trees. The view was spectacular, particularly looking out from the stone balcony, which in spring was dressed in drooping fragrant panicles of light blue wisteria. The building was ramshackle, with no bathroom or toilet. Leah and Bobbie had no money to spare for such additions and relied on an old-fashioned soil toilet—nipping out to the garden at night and in the mornings and whenever necessary in between. Chamber pots for those snow-bound times.

Even so, such friendships take time. In those early days, Sarah wasn't just seeking people who spoke English. She was seeking the comfort of someone who might at least understand the deeper meaning behind her words. Without a network of work friends or nearby family, those everyday connections people make in their daily lives, Sarah was alone and having to remake her life, to make it recognisable. A lot of the time, it seemed like make believe.

And with the addition of the uncomfortable presence of the angry neighbour, it also verged on the nightmarish—a looking-glass world where you can't interpret the attitudes and gestures of other humans, because they don't mean what you think they mean.

CHAPTER 8 *bis*

I remember when I first moved to France from the UK back in the 1970s. I was a modern foreign languages student; this was to be my 'year abroad,' part of the studies for my undergraduate degree. My posting as an *assistante d'anglais* (English teaching assistant) was to *'un coin perdu'* (a lost corner) as the locals called it, in the southern Midi region of France. My lodging was on the school premises, a seven-storey dun-coloured municipal building, a half-boarding school that housed boys and girls all week, but was empty on the weekend, when the children returned home, if they were lucky, or to other institutions if they had no family. My room on the third floor contained a single iron bedstead and mattress, a sink and an iron wardrobe. Everything clanged. The window overlooked the main street that wound down and away from me, flanked by two lines of plane trees, their leaves drooping under the autumn rain.

I was equipped with nine years of learning French. Could I open my mouth and expect anything coherent to emerge? One of the English teachers addressed me on my first day in school. I only completed half a sentence because I couldn't form the correct verb tense in time to say it in response. Instead, I stayed silent. Partly, I was held back by the need for perfection because of the style of language teaching that I had experienced, partly I was held back by shyness, partly I was held back by sheer fear. I didn't know how to speak any more. I felt like an idiot. No one would know who I was.

That feeling lasted for several months. It was only after a short break, spent communicating only in my native English, that the puzzle pieces of the French language started to fall into place quickly enough for them to emerge in the right order from my mouth. My brain needed that break to assimilate the new information, to order it, to make sense of it. The moment I realised that this had happened was at a dinner with French friends. We were sitting at the table, they were chatting away as usual; I was trying to chew the food while rapidly processing all the possible shapes in which my French sentences might make their entrance. And then, suddenly, my mouth made sounds I hadn't practised in my head first prior to delivery. The sentence flew into the centre of the table, hovered above it then joined the rest of the conversation. My first completely unrehearsed utterance. It was magic. I had cracked it. From then on, French was my best and most glamorous friend.

CHAPTER 9
Un cane in Chiesa
(or The worm in the Apple)

Piedmont
Summer 2004

...He was like a shadow. He would appear without sound and then complain. I felt at times like an animal in a cage, as he would prowl the borders staring to see what we were doing... you never knew he was there until he growled at you. Even if you caught his eye, he would go on glaring and say nothing, forcing us (mainly me) to look the other way. (From Sarah's notes)

The two cats were there again at the top of the driveway, next to the house. Sarah saw them as she was walking back up from the road that runs past the bottom of the driveway, after waving goodbye to Luke. Three days ahead of her without him. There was much to do, the time would pass quickly, she would be too tired to worry about the night-time.

Sarah was used to being alone—even before she started travelling for her job and certainly before she and Luke lived together and moved to Italy.

As the youngest child of four, she became caught up in the drama of her mother's life. Her father was a deputy head teacher and had numerous responsibilities that took him out in the evening. Her older siblings had already left home by the time their grandmother developed dementia and needed care. When her mother left the house every evening at nine o'clock to look after her, Sarah was often on her own. The baby of the family, but the one of whom the most was demanded.

'I've always been left on my own. And at night. As a child, I probably was scared,' Sarah says, but if anyone asks her about being scared in the Italian house, she dismisses it: *'I can't be scared. I can't live if I'm scared.'*

The cats were staring at her, sitting on their pale haunches, each carefully licking a velvety purple paw as if considering their next move. As Sarah drew nearer, they rose from the gritty surface, stretched in unison, then disappeared silently into the hazelnut grove. The leaves on the trees were already brittle brown and falling at the height of summer. The only sound was the crackling of the fallen leaves under their delicate tread.

Sarah thought of her neighbour. He had become *il Cattivo*, the Nasty One. The cats were just like him, always sneaking around and then turning up in some unexpected spot to startle her. They weren't like any cats she had known. They certainly weren't like her beloved Cinnamon. Before she even realised it, Sarah was crying. Not just for her dead cat, but for the life she had long left behind, the English garden, full of flat-headed achillea, tall deep-pink penstemon, pillar-box red salvia and the delphiniums that kept falling over and being eaten by snails. And her favourites, the lupins, which the snails also loved, but over which Sarah kept a special vigil.

And now here she was, on a northern Italian mountaintop, cultivating soil that was so different from the black crumbly compost of her old garden. It is sandy and dry and yellow. The things that grow in it have leaves the colour of dust—the rosemary, the thyme and the gnarly olive trees. They smell of sun and heat, not of rain and green grass.

Enough. She shook her narrow shoulders; this was just sentimental self-indulgence. She quickened her pace towards the gate that now guards her courtyard. As Sarah rounded the corner of her house and slid in through the partially open solid sheet of two-metre-high black-painted steel, she saw that the huge terracotta pot, full of perfect, unmolested basil, was lying on its side, in pieces.

Sarah knelt to look at the damage. Too big for a cat to knock over—had *il Cattivo* been sniffing around. Did he know she was alone? She glanced over her shoulder, then looked down at the broken pieces of pottery. She picked up one of the bigger shards of terracotta and ran her index finger over the sharp point.

Sarah slipped through the curtain of insect-repelling plastic strips hanging in the back door entrance (bowing to the demands of utility over beauty) and entered the house. It was dark and cool after the bright, heavy heat of the courtyard. She waited for her eyes to adjust, then moved from the kitchen to the living room, her hand tight around the shard. Everything was so dark, so still. The only window was in the permanent shadow of the hazelnut grove. The room was used in the evening to watch the TV; otherwise it remained empty. Sarah turned to the stairs—stone, stone-cold—and started up towards the bedrooms. Nothing. No one. Of course not.

As she headed back down the stairs, Sarah realised she had not locked the big metal gate, installed to keep out *il Cattivo* and his two Belgian Shepherds, large wolf-like dogs with pointed muzzles and ears to match,

Out in the dazzle, the gate was standing ajar. Sarah ran to it, slid the bolts into place, stood back. She was still clutching the shard. As she turned, intending to head into the terraced garden that falls away below the courtyard, Sarah saw the two cats sitting side by side on the low wall that separates the courtyard from the stretch of land where the apricot trees grow. They were staring up at her intensely.

Sarah discovered that she had raised her hand, the one holding the shard. Are the cats programmed to stare at me like that? Are they relaying pictures to *il Cattivo?* Are they *spying* on me?

She threw the shard. The cats ran away, squealing, their mushroom-coloured tails moving angrily from side to side.

Sarah went over to the wall where they had been sitting. She had never hurt an animal in her life. What was she doing?

*

'*Bastardo.*'

Il Cattivo was throwing stones at Luke while screaming at him.

'*Che cavolo è?*' (What the hell?)

He didn't seem to care who he hit with the bits of scree he was grabbing up from the ground and launching into the air, along with a bunch of tasty swear words.

'*Bastardo*' was now *il Cattivo's* customary title for Luke, Sarah said. They always thought of their neighbour as *il Cattivo* now; they could barely remember his real name. (This was the word scrawled on the sign telling them to shut the gate, their gate, when they had first bought the house, before they moved here. They didn't recognise it, could find it nowhere in any dictionary.) He had a name for Sarah too. Whenever she got back from some outing, a bike ride, a trip into town, he greeted her with *testa di cazzo è tornata* ('dickhead is back').

On this occasion, Luke was still furious and upset. That cat, that bloody awful cat of *Cattivo's*, had attacked their timid little cat *Basilico* again. Luke had chased the cat off their land and into the driveway, hotly disputed turf, and still *il Cattivo* was pelting him with gravel. Luke retreated, walking back through the high metal gate, now semi-hidden under trails of variegated ivy (he and Sarah were so relieved the ivy now covered the gate, it felt less like they were in some kind of prison compound). The gate clanged shut.

The gate, its clanging, always seemed to inspire intense anger in the neighbour, this small, ageing, ferocious bow-legged man with the oddly bulky upper body.

They had already been forced to go the police about the dogs. They were kept on the balcony, the roof of the lower part of the house next door, around which they paced, barking all the time. (I remember this from my first visit in 2003, I felt nervous, but also sorry for them, ranging around with all that pent-up strength on a bare roof in the heat). They used to escape sometimes. Rumours circulated that they had killed a local dog, but no one had made a complaint, which made Luke angry.

Daisy was visiting in the spring of that year, 2004— before they had installed the metal gate. The only thing separating the two houses was the dirt road, the tail end of the driveway. Luke had parked the car well over to the side of the road, the side of the hazelnut grove, squeezing in as tight to the edge of the driveway as possible. He didn't want trouble.

'In you get Mum.' He gestured to the car door he was holding open for Daisy. She was in a happy mood. She had arrived at this wonderful place a few days ago, one of her regular visits, to which she always looked forward, and particularly this year after the long, grey winter in England. It was so lovely and warm; she didn't need a jacket, nor even a sweater to sling over her shoulders. She wore just a shirt—her favourite faded red and blue check—and the cotton twill trousers. As she walked towards her son, a flurry of barking started. The Belgian shepherds had come down—somehow—from the roof and were in front of her, baring their sharp yellow teeth, scummy with plaque, their black lips drawn back.

Daisy recognised angry dogs when she saw them, but they were blocking her path to the car. Luke was momentarily stunned. He didn't move. But just as he unfroze and started to aim a kick at the dogs, *il Cattivo* emerged from the shade of the wall. He barked something at them, grabbed each dog by the collar, adroitly avoiding their teeth, then hauled them in behind the wall of the next-door property.

He did not reappear. No apologies. No placatory gesture.

The dogs escaped several times in those first months they were at *Cascina Cannella;* furious, powerless, Sarah and Luke watched them roam across the slope down by the apricot trees, sniff around the vines, cock their legs against the house wall. They could not bear it.

They had to confront *il Cattivo*.

'*Non ho visto niente, non ho visto niente,*' he growled. He was behind the house; he didn't see anything.

'*Non è successo niente, non è successo niente.*' He continued to deny that the dogs had been roaming on Luke and Sarah's land; nothing happened, nothing happened.

But Luke was not going to be beaten. The next time he caught sight of the dogs pissing all over their land, he took pictures. *Il Cattivo* would not be able to deny the truth.

The municipal police station was a brutalist grey concrete structure, in contrast to the other buildings in town, painted in yellows and creams and dull pinks and glowing against the cloudless blue of the sky. When Luke showed the pictures of the free-ranging dogs to the *Commissario*, who was a man in his fifties, slightly grizzled and not unkind, he won a first victory. (The *Commissario* soon moved on from this small town; he was wiser and swifter than the local recruits.) A fence appeared along the boundary of *il Cattivo's* property, presumably after some persuasion from the police chief. Luke is not a demonstrative man, but this was a sweet moment. It was now clear how to deal with this neighbour—get the evidence, prove your case.

Meanwhile, *il Cattivo's* cats continued to use the territory around *Cascina Cannella* as their own private turf. And not only the land.

'They used to come into the house and they peed in the house and they pooed in the house, these cats,' says Sarah.

When we talk about *il Cattivo*, it doesn't matter how much time has passed since the incidents, Sarah is always completely back in the moment of it, feeling again that intense frustration at a situation she does not understand and cannot control. How can someone be this irrational, this *angry?*

'In your *house?*' I repeat, stupidly.

'It's almost as if they'd been sent in. I honestly thought they had a tape recorder on them or something.'

'It sounds bizarre, but at the height of all this (the neighbour wars) we were just convinced they were spying on us, because they were just so nasty. I mean, I love cats, but...' Luke tails off. Luke is serious, which is surprising. He is the one who usually tries to damp down Sarah's flights of imagination. 'Sarah is such a good person. Who would want to upset her?'

There is a picture of Amy, Luke's young niece, playing with *il Cattivo's* cat when it was a kitten. It was taken just after he and Sarah had moved to Italy for good. They might have left England, but England hadn't forgotten them. Relatives were wasting little time visiting them, anxious to see this remote and beautiful place Luke and Sarah had fetched up.

'She was lovely with *Cattivo's* cat. But once we got our own two cats, *Basilico* and *Rosmarino,* all the neighbour's cats got very territorial. They attacked *Basilico*, got him in the eye with a claw. Blinded him. He had the most beautiful blue eyes, didn't he?' Luke looks at Sarah. They look at each other. Both cats are now dead.

Basilico is basil in Italian; *Rosmarino* is rosemary. Luke and Sarah have used spice and herb names for all the animals they have collected—and lost—over the years they have lived at *Cascina Cannella.*

They tried hard not to let their neighbour's behaviour affect them, or their feelings about their home. And it continued to be a dream, even as the feud metastasized, creeping into every corner of their lives. They tended the land—spraying the vineyard and fruit trees, watering the vegetables, weeding, mulching, planting. The got on with the rebuilding and renovating of the house, with the planning for the future. But *il Cattivo* was always there, lurking, waiting for an opportunity to insert himself into their lives.

Sarah in particular suffered from the neighbour's snooping and complaining, because she too was always there.

She found him creepy. She would feel a presence behind her, never announced, never a '*Buongiorno*,' just a... kind of hovering.

Sarah felt keenly the pressure of his surveillance. When she had to leave the house, returning was fraught with tension.

'If I used to see him wandering, I'd wander around for the next half an hour, waiting for him to go, to disappear, before I could return home,' Sarah says. 'He made me feel quite sick, quite ill. He was quite an imposing figure.'

*

Italian inheritance laws are such that a property gets divided amongst all the relatives. In the case of the house next door, there had been a protracted process of figuring out who had rights to what. Luke and Sarah dug around, talked to other people in the neighbourhood and managed to find out some of the history. *Il Cattivo* did not own the house. Apparently, the owner had died in the 1980s, leaving a wife who did not feel happy nor safe enough to live in such a big house by herself and so had left it empty and moved back in with her brother and sister 'at the grand old age of seventy.'

'So it seems that you're never too old to move back home,' Sarah remarks.

She had only been married for one year before her husband died and had not inherited all of the property, but the major percentage, according to Italian law. Another fourteen family members also had rights. How can you get fourteen people to agree? For years, the house had remained empty as the fourteen discussed what to do with it.

'Should they sell it or leave it to rot, as a sort of shrine to their ancestors, as most Italians appear to do?' Sarah explains that as time went by, some of the fourteen died and they then left their portion to their relatives. The web grew more and more complicated until it was so complicated not even the family knew who owned a piece of the house.

Il Cattivo had a wife and two daughters. His wife was one of the fourteen who had inherited part of the next-door property, as a granddaughter. She and *il Cattivo* were living in a rented apartment and were very interested in obtaining the whole house. One rumour about *il Cattivo* and his wife that greatly pleases Sarah and Luke is that they had once been very rich, but had lost it all in the casinos in San Remo (known as Italy's Monte Carlo).

However, no one could agree on a price, so they were given permission by the other descendants/inheritors to use the house as a temporary property.

'The *Cattivi* (the whole family were now Nasty Ones) hoped to own it completely one day.' Apparently, they were desperate to own a property—'but not desperate enough to pay the asking price the others wanted,' says Sarah. So the waiting game continued and each year, the house became more and more ruined as water and damp entered the roof.

According to the gossip, Sarah and Luke discovered that *il Cattivo* did not get on with the rest of the inheritors, probably because he had once asked them to give their share of the house to him as a gift. This was a double insult: one, to think that he, a non-member of the family, should be entitled to the house free of charge; and two, that the house was, in fact, worthless. This was not the way to win friends, so the issue of buying the house was even more problematic than it should have been, as both groups would not talk directly to each other. Somehow—Sarah and Luke are not sure of the details—the couple managed to obtain the largest share in the house, giving them power over the other shareholders. There was no love lost. *Il Cattivo* became a figure of hate.

Sarah and Luke had a surprise visit in August 2004—a year after the big move. A very angry seventy-seven-year-old man with white hair and eyes like raisins in folds of weather-beaten skin, turned up on their doorstep. He was part of the inheritance group, now swollen to about eighteen people because of various deaths. The older person would pass his or her portion on to the next generation. At one point, a share of the pie was passed to someone under five years old and a guardian was appointed.

Their visitor lived a fair distance away, twenty or thirty kilometres. He had come to check on the house, which had still not been sold to *il Cattivo*, even though the family was living there. It was evident he wanted to have a good rant about them.

In the past, they had arguments over rights of way; *Cattivo's* courtyard was part owned by this angry white-haired man. Ultimately, they swapped rights of way—but he never ceased to hate Cattivo, *'voglio guidare la mia macchina nel cortile di Cattivo e distruggerlo.'* (I want to drive my car right through *Cattivo's* courtyard and destroy it). He even called him *Cattivo,* not knowing that this was the name Sarah and Luke had chosen for their troublesome neighbour. The old man included the dead fig trees in his list of grievances—they had toppled over one night in fearsome winds. He also grumbled about the hazelnuts scattered on the ground that hadn't been gathered.

'Unfortunately for us, we had arrived right in the middle of this family feud as our land was completely encircled by next door,' says Sarah.

'They—the *Cattivi*—thought they were important. She's always turned out very beautifully, she makes up her eyes. Pretty curly hair, grey. She doesn't dye it. She always wears white clothes, even though she doesn't have the figure to wear these tight jeans.' Sarah is lean as a whippet, and these days, lipstick is about the most artificial thing she applies to her face, so most people are plump and decorated compared to her.

Il Cattivo drove a BMW, which he brought up and down the hill every day from his apartment to the house next door. A grand tour of 8km. They were really an unlikely couple in the country hills, says Sarah.

'Here, everyone has worked all their lives; they drive in battered Pandas and only wear their best clothes on Sundays or festival days. A BMW was out of place in these hills of narrow roads. When *Signora Cattivo* went to work in the vineyard with pink rubber gloves and a white jumper, the locals laughed. They were like children playing at being farmers, driving a small noisy tractor which resembled Thomas the Tank Engine.'

*

Piedmont
The present

The four of us, Luke and Sarah, Daisy and me, are seated in our usual spot, the balcony at the end of the house that looks out over the hillside. Dinner is over. We are still savouring the flavours of this meal of several courses—shrimp in homemade mayonnaise, followed by ricotta and spinach gnocchi, cornmeal bread to mop up, all finished off with pears stewed in wine accompanied by homemade hazelnut ice cream. Yum!

It is dark, our faces illuminated only by starlight and the flame of a small candle in the centre of the table. It feels excitingly spooky.

Il Cattivo didn't like it when some time in 2004 Sarah and Luke installed windows on the back wall of the house overlooking the gloomy hazelnut grove, this scrap of land that lies at the root of all the troubles.

'The law says if you don't have any land behind your house, you can't open windows overlooking the land,' explained Sarah. 'So if those two metres behind our house were ours, then we could open the windows, but if they weren't ours then he might be... slightly right. The compromise was that we used opaque glass.'

Was the argument with *il Cattivo* about these two metres of earth—was that in part because of Sarah and Luke's inability to explain properly that they understood it to be *their* land? Was it because *il Cattivo* just didn't *understand* them? Was it because they just didn't understand *il Cattivo?*

The controversy heated up because of the windows.

'Sarah found herself playing Keystone Kops with *il Cattivo.'*

'They're fixed windows, so how do you clean them?'

'Well,' Luke said, smiling wryly, part of the double act, 'of course you have to go onto the land around the back of the house.'

'I'd creep round to the back of the house when he wasn't here, skim up a ladder, quickly clean them, then skim back round.' We all grin at the image. But Sarah isn't joining in.

'Seriously, that's what I'd do. And when I really hated him, because I did, I had to wait until he was gone, quickly get the ladder out...'

'You could see it in a movie, couldn't you,' I say, too flippantly. The surrounding darkness of the night is contributing to our sense of how unnerving it was to live in fear of *il Cattivo* materialising when you thought you were alone. I glance over my shoulder, involuntarily.

'In fact one day, the cat climbed up the ladder after me. Total panic.'

After a moment, Sarah says, 'So you can see why he did get cross, because he thought the land was his. It's a no-man's land now.'

They had to communicate with him through the *geometra*. This is what Luke and Sarah call their architect/site manager/building engineer—the person who knows the right people to deal with in the bureaucracy and can navigate the ways round tricky regulations. They use the word *geometra* because it has no exact equivalent in English. It's what happens when you live in a culture not your own; you take the most appropriate word from the language rather than trying to translate it—there may not be an equivalent.

There was one snag, however, in that this particular *geometra* was also scared of *il Cattivo*, who made his low opinion of the *geometra* clear when their paths crossed—'*non vale niente*' (useless); '*non sa la legge*' (he doesn't know the law). And to Sarah, who was trying so hard to learn Italian so that she could communicate effectively—for this, she believed, was one of the principal reasons *il Cattivo* was so intransigent—he had this to say: '*Stai creando sempre dei problemi. Perché non stai zitta?*' (You're always trying to cause trouble. Why don't you keep quiet?)

*

I will survive

Bath
Green shutters
External door designs
Fire buying
Cinghiale (wild boar)
Calabrone (hornet)
Cattivo (Mr Nasty)
and the fruit

SURVIVAL

Washing
Candles, wet cement and wooden struts

This list, found in Sarah's notes, is perhaps an indicator of just how uncharacteristically scattershot and random her thoughts were in those early months. And the item in capital letters on the list is like a shout for help. Perhaps Sarah didn't even know she was shouting...

CHAPTER 9 *bis*

Due ricette di Luke

Antipasto (starter)
 Peeled shrimp with chunks of avocado, dressed with homemade mayonnaise, with lemon juice.

Il primo (first course)
 Ricotta and spinach gnocchi with a sauce made from preserved tomatoes

 200gm spinach
 Parsley leaves
 1 garlic clove
 140gm ricotta
 85gm plain flour
 2 eggs
 100gm Parmesan cheese (plus extra to sprinkle)
 Nutmeg

Luke boils or steams the spinach, wrings it very dry, then mixes up all the ingredients in a large bowl. He forms them into small balls and freezes them (or just refrigerates them for half an hour if he wants to use them right away). To cook them, he boils some water and drops in about eight-ten of the balls at a time. When they are ready, they rise to the top. After about another minute, he takes them out. He serves them with a tomato sauce from their collection of over 400 jars of preserves.

I had a sudden revelation that Italian cookery is, in essence, very simple and Luke agreed with me. It is all about the quality of the ingredients.

CHAPTER 10
Along came Peter

'First of all, the old terra (soil) had to be removed from between the stones. This terra had been mixed with Moscato (wine) when the house had been built originally, as wine was more plentiful than water because the house was situated on top of a hill, and had no well. Consequently, the terra was very sticky and it was understandable why, throughout the summer, we had a type of wasp burrowing into this sweet sticky stuff to make a nest.'

(From Sarah's notes)

It was the summer of 2005. An enormous battered old car, a cherry red 1960 Pontiac Catalina convertible, swung around the corner of the front courtyard of *Cascina Cannella* as deftly as if the driver were manoeuvring a Vespa scooter. Peter had arrived.

His spiky haircut, *'fatto in casa'* was homemade— hairdressing was only one of his many skills, as Sarah learnt. On his top lip, there was a tattooed beauty spot, acquired when he was a sailor. His ears were pierced, and his eyebrows were very pointed, giving him a permanently surprised look. He wore a pencil thin beard along the sharp jut of his jaw. As Sarah greeted him, she was enveloped in a haze of strong aftershave.

The name Peter is an Anglicisation of his Albanian name. He came to *Cascina Cannella* via the recommendation of the *geometra*. He had been working in Italy many years, doing all types of manual jobs. His father had also been a builder and was Peter's teacher, passing on to him the skills and knowledge he had gained.

Cascina Cannella had not been occupied, in total, for eleven years by the time Sarah and Luke moved in permanently. When they bought this semi-derelict house in a faraway place, it had been abandoned for eight years. After the purchase, for three years the house was still essentially uninhabited. It was primarily a building site, occupied only by Sarah and Luke for periods of weeks at a time, or, unofficially, by builders working on the site.

Sarah and I are spending a pleasant morning looking at the photo albums containing the backbreaking history of the renovations. And it does seem like history now. It is a shock to see the original state of the house, returning slowly and gracefully to its constituent parts: the dust falling from the rotting wooden beams; the damp and the dirt taking the earthenware tiles back into the heart of the earth; flakes of plaster and stone littering the ground; gaps like missing teeth in the chewed-up bricks. It is post-breakfast, but pre-lunch, which I am anticipating with great pleasure because of the large, bright red, juicy tomatoes I observed being plucked by Luke fresh from the vine this morning. These are the last tomatoes from the garden and are, in Daisy's words, 'red all the way through.'

There was nothing ordinary about Peter. He blew into their lives, banishing the shadow of *il Cattivo*—at least, for a time. Luke was away working during that period, earning the bread-and-butter money essential to keeping the project afloat. While he travelled, Sarah threw herself wholeheartedly into the renovations. She became well versed in different building techniques and acquired a variety of skills. How far all this was from her pre-Italy life. But as time went on, she found she didn't miss the Sarah she once was. She didn't miss her at all.

Sarah the builder

The walls on either side of the stone staircase, which led up from the main door, were bare of plaster. The first building team had either stripped it off or chunks of it had fallen

128

here and there over the years. No marvellous old frescoes were revealed. Bare stones were left, pockmarked and crumbly. Walking upstairs felt like climbing the turret of a 'spooky castle,' says Sarah. These stones could not be reclaimed. They would have to be re-plastered.

Not all skills are equal. Plastering, for example. Sarah quite quickly realised, as she worked alongside Peter, that she would never get to grips with plastering—although she did learn the importance of keeping it wet. Water was hosed continuously down the walls, leaving streams cascading down the stairs. It was Sarah's job to clean this. She wore nothing but grubby cotton t-shirts and drawstring trousers or shorts. Her figure was like a line drawing when set against the picture of Peter in dark singlet and shorts, revealing fiercely muscular limbs.

While Sarah was nominally the *capo*, the boss, she was, in essence, Peter's assistant. He treated her as an assistant too —a nineteenth century artist with a nineteenth century attitude to women, although perhaps not many women acted as builders' mates in nineteenth century Piedmont.

'*La vita e dura, la vita e molto dura.*' (Life is hard, life is very hard,) was Peter's constant lament.

Sarah groaned to herself every time he reiterated this sad refrain. Her Italian was still shaky at this point. They were communicating in what she thought of as 'foreigner Italian'—a stew of Italian words let loose in a hit and miss fashion in the hope of conveying meaning, each word following the other in a stream of complicated, but friendly effort. Sarah soon got fed up with Peter's range of 'it's a hard life' refrains, so she taught him to say them in English for more variety. This proved diverting, particularly when they started working in closer proximity and on a more equal footing. Once they had finished the plastering, life took a turn for the more interesting. Sarah was promoted from cleaner to co-worker. The job was to repoint the walls of the bedroom, where the Madonna's stern image had once terrorised Sarah's mother-in-law Daisy, and to repoint the ceilings.

'This seemed like a simple job, but it turned into an epic with me playing a starring role,' she says now.

Before they could repoint the stonework, Sarah and Peter had to prepare it by removing the old material holding the stones together. At *Cascina Cannella*, this material was not the usual mortar you might expect to be made from a mix containing cement and water, but something much more exotic, soil, or *terra*, mixed with Moscato wine.

Repointing was painstaking. Side by side they stood on their respective ladders, patiently working at the stones in semi-darkness, the only light coming through the window apertures. Peter carved each stone into a more regular shape, so the new grout would fit easily between the stones. He was like a mountain goat, nimbly climbing his ladder, stretching across the walls to reach particular areas. And all you could hear were the sounds of chisel and hammer, chipping at the old *terra*, shaping the stones. Stone and *terra* flew everywhere. Peter liked singing while he worked. He was a singer in his spare time, he told Sarah, although she could not imagine how he managed to fit singing into his life—it seemed to her he worked all the time.

The building site became a particular, intense, highly focused world with its sounds and smells. The chipping of the stones, the exasperated buzzings of the wasps, Peter's tenor tones. His heady aftershave mingled with the sour old *terra* mortar, the not unpleasant scent of human sweat created from hard physical labour, and the occasional fleeting whiff of rosemary or thyme carried on the light breeze from the garden. The two of them flung wet cement into the gaps, used wire brushes to remove the excess. Then they turned the hosepipe onto the walls, standing side by side as they watched the water cascade, taking away the debris, revealing the sleek surfaces of the renewed stones.

It was not only painstaking work, but also exhausting. They worked every day except Sundays for a month. Sarah found muscles in her body she hadn't known existed. While her muscles doubled in size, her body became pared down almost to the bone. But once they had varnished the ceiling bricks, the result was fantastic. Sarah felt the walls and ceilings were works of art. So did Peter. He was so very particular about every detail that everything took three times as long as the original estimate. Sarah had no quarrel with this. She and Peter were in tune, each as demanding of attention to detail as the other. At moments, while each was on their ladder, straining to scrape out the old *terra*, Sarah would catch Peter's eye. They would grin at each other. It was a peaceful kind of contentment. *Il Cattivo* had been pushed into the background; he was nothing more than one of those irritating wasps, a pest to be swatted away, at least for now…

'Peter was a perfectionist, an artist in full flow, a maestro,' she says admiringly. 'He had been warned we were very fussy about the standard of the work, but so was he, and he wasn't concerned about working for us.'

Sarah had introduced Peter to the British habit of drinking a cup of tea in the afternoon. Even this did not slow him down. 'He would drink a mug of hot liquid in two minutes flat, unwilling to be away from the work for too long.'

She was happier than she had ever been back in the UK —indeed, she could hardly imagine any more the life she had led there. Here, life was utterly purposeful. There was physical work to be done and she was the one who had not only to organise and oversee it, but, being Sarah, had also to take full part in it. She wanted to get her hands dirty, to be fully involved in shaping the house that was going to be not only her and Luke's home, but also a reflection of how they saw themselves, a vindication of their choice of a way of life that was both unconventional and demanding.

131

This wasn't about getting themselves a fancy Italian farmhouse, made beautiful by the hard work of others, or living a luxurious life in the Italian countryside, removed from the reality of modern living. They weren't simply 'second homers,' or outsiders dipping a toe into someone else's culture and taking out the good bits. They were in it for life.

*

Peter and Sarah fell into the habit of eating lunch together. Sarah's old food technology past caught up with her when she noticed Peter relied on packaged food a lot—dried risotto with added water.

She warned him about monosodium glutamate. It's not something you would think of in rural Piedmont—the dangers of fast food. But here was Sarah, a foreigner, teaching Peter, a long-term inhabitant of Italy, about how to eat more healthily.

'Really Peter, you can't eat that,' she instructed him bossily. He responded with a nonchalant shrug, curving his lips into a beguiling smile, his beauty spot dimpling. Sarah could not help but grin back, as he perched on an old foldup metal chair in front of her, scooping moistened risotto into his mouth, while she stood watching him, hands sternly on hips.

One day, instead of bringing a packet of ready-made food to work, Peter turned up with some local sausage, alongside a packet of dried pasta. He presented them to Sarah with an operatic trill of his tenor voice.

From that moment, *Cascina Cannella* became a restaurant, offering dried pasta, maybe a tin of tuna or a sausage, or the ultimate ingredient—two little frozen fishes. Peter always came to work with surprise ingredients tucked away in his bag.

'What is the restaurant serving today for you *Capo*?' he would ask Sarah, before revealing his offerings with a flourish.

*

The relationship between Sarah and Peter shifted. Sarah was still the c*apo*, but Peter began to boss her around. It started with the cement. Peter was scathing. *'Il cemento è troppo molle. Non eri concentrata quando l'hai fatto, stavi pensando alle pulizia.'* (The cement is too thin. You were not concentrating when you made it, you were thinking of cleaning.)

Sarah didn't like this. She was confused, but couldn't express her thoughts precisely to Peter. She also hated it when he said: *'Sei capace de fare?'* (Can you do it?) Sarah felt she was being condescended to, as if he were saying: 'Are you capable of doing it?' Of course she was capable. Peter was being just like Luke used to be when they had started out on the renovations. If she tried unsuccessfully to hammer a nail into a wall, Luke assumed it was Sarah's weakness that caused her to fail. Not so. She enjoyed her triumph when Luke, too, failed to penetrate these walls with his hammer and his nail.

'The secret,' Sarah always says, 'was to forget what you knew from growing up in redbrick houses in England.' The *cascina* was built from stone with walls sometimes half a metre thick.

'Even putting up a picture involved getting out the drill,' she remembers. Before she and Peter started the renovations in earnest, Sarah had already done a lot of empirical research—that is, spent time talking to local people about how to do things. 'Everyone had their own ideas,' she says. It was simply a case of deciding from the long list of options what method to choose.

'Even after I had finished a room, the Italians would always tell me how I should have done something differently.' Sarah chuckles when she tells me this. She is used to being second-guessed by all manner of knowledgeable men.

With Peter, the problem was that Sarah had mixed feelings about how he spoke to her. She was a woman, after all, and he seemed to forget that she might not be as strong as him, and therefore, not take her properly into account.

'Did he *forget* I was a woman?'

And yet, Sarah also was proud of her increasing strength, liked it. In short, she wanted to have her cake and eat it (or, as the Italian idiom has it in its own inimitable way: *avere la botte piena e la moglie ubriaca*—to have a full barrel and a drunk wife).

And she did indeed get her revenge one day.

'Cos'è successo ai tuoi muscoli?' (What's happened to your muscles?) Peter taunted her, when she asked him to carry something for her. She then handed him the copper drainpipe for reattachment. When he asked if it was heavy, she replied no. She watched with satisfaction as he nearly dropped it...

A sweet moment. The balance of power had shifted again.

Renovation in earnest...

Sarah and Luke were exhilarated by the success of the renovation of the interior stonework. They were in love with the building. The beauty of the work they had done made them anxious about all the potential beauty they could create. It weighed on Sarah. She became haunted by the possibilities of even greater achievements. It is an odd thing, being haunted by the potential of beauty, of perfection. It's not rational. It's almost an obsession. Sarah found herself in the grips of it. Which is why she decided to use her newly acquired repointing skills on the *outside* of the house, with Peter as her partner in ambition.

134

Sarah admits she lost her senses completely at this point. *Cascina Cannella* was in control of her life. She decided, with Peter, that they should repoint the whole of the outside of the house, which was at that time covered in old, crumbling, decrepit buttermilk plaster. This was going to be more than a month's work.

In fact, it turned into four months' work, which they carried out through a long, cold, *Piemontese* winter of snow banks and rapidly decreasing wood piles. A Piedmont winter has to be prepared for. Temperatures can fall to near zero Celsius in January and February and snow can arrive in astounding quantities.

'Some days it was so cold your ears felt like they were in a freezer, and the work was hard,' says Sarah.

Removing the plaster was not straightforward. As Sarah and Peter chipped it off, they uncovered more and more surprises. Ghosts of doors and windows long blocked up. When the house was built, each room would have had four windows or doors—*each* room.

The houses in this part of rural Italy are not cosy, but large, thick-walled and serious. *Cascina Cannella*, however, with its many openings, now hidden under the plaster coating, turned out not to be so solidly constructed. It was fortuitous Sarah's quest for perfection led them to find out what was hiding under the old plaster.

Cascina Cannella's previous owner had filled up the holes badly with whatever he could find—including razor blades, glass, old floor tiles...

Peter was removing a stone one day, when, to his surprise, soil poured out of the side of the house. Mice had played their part in building the house too. They had made many nests in various holes in the walls. These badly filled openings in the house walls had to be cleared out before they could be blocked up again, this time with artistically arranged stones. Consequently, parts of the house became unstable as each opening was cleared of its strange contents. Nevertheless, the work was not just hard slog and backbreaking. Nor was it dispiriting. Creating stone patterns to refill these window and door openings consumed Sarah and Peter with delight.

'Peter became Picasso at work,' says Sarah, smiling to herself at the memory of his 'artistic temperament.'

She mixed over a tonne of cement by hand. They had a good routine. She helped to pass the cement up the scaffolding to Peter, then climbed the scaffolding to help him clean the stones. However, it was Peter's skill that thrilled them both.

'*Quando sarà finita, la gente fermerà la macchina per guardare la casa. Diventerà un museo,*' (When it is finished, people will stop the car to look at the house. It will be a museum,) he proclaimed at the end of most days, standing back and admiring their work, running his hands though his hair and leaving behind little bits of cement and debris. The house was becoming more and more solid, more and more beautiful.

'*À dire il vero,*' he said, '*dovrebbero pagare per l'entrata.*' Peter thought they should charge an entrance fee to view the house.

*

None of this pleased the neighbour.

'*Spero che la casa non crolla,*' he would repeat to Sarah every time their paths crossed, although she thought he probably meant the opposite: that he hoped the house *would* fall down.

Peter took pleasure in teasing *il Cattivo*. When she was with Peter, Sarah was able to bank down her dread of him appearing out of nowhere. She wasn't constantly checking the courtyard for a glimpse of him, or listening from the top of the vineyard to detect the tell-tale whine of *Cattivo's* tractor underneath the soft soughing of the breeze from the hillside. Instead, she attacked the stones to the accompaniment of Peter's quirky adaptation of some half-remembered Verdi aria. Life was indeed bliss.

When they removed the rotting beams, Peter would shout to *il Cattivo* from the top of the scaffolding, '*Metto due pietre nel muro, e quattro cadano.*' (I put two stones back, and four drop out.)

One brittle morning, dry and wintry, the wind blowing across the courtyard just enough to chill them to the bone, but not to disturb their materials, the scaffolding started to shake. *Il Cattivo* was squatting on his tractor, driving it through the courtyard (*not* his land, *not* his right). He brushed by the scaffolding, touching the precarious construction with his tractor. Sarah was standing on it, several metres above ground, cleaning each stone by hand. Of course, neither she nor Peter was wearing a harness. It was simply a question of hanging on to the nearest scaffolding pipe.

'*Tieni forte,*' Peter wasn't laughing this time. He cried out in a panic, grabbing a piece of scaffolding, but Sarah clapped her hands together slowly in a round of applause. She was *not* going to show that man how frightened she was. Afterwards, Peter was all for going around to the neighbour's house and killing him, or at least giving him a serious fright. Sarah talked him out of his fury—she had to live next door to this man, after all—but inside, her spirits were dancing at Peter's roaring rage. It went some way to assuaging her dread of *il Cattivo*.

Both she and Peter lost three kilos while working on the house. By Easter of 2006, they needed a break, even though it was not finished. Peter went back to Albania to sort out his (complicated) love life and Sarah returned to 'normal' life at *Cascina Cannella*—but Peter did not leave without a parting gift.

*

Peter was a gifted sculptor. On only the third occasion Sarah met him, he brought two pieces of his work to show her. One was a man sitting on a chair drinking beer, carved in intricate detail. The second was significantly different. Peter warned Sarah that it was *sporco*—dirty. And he didn't mean that it needed a good clean. It was a graphic carving of a man and woman having sex, with the man behind the woman. The wooden lady looked a bit taken aback. So did Sarah. She turned the carving over quickly to find a huge pair of breasts looking at her…

She wasn't sure how to react. In life before Italy, she had been a professional woman maintaining friendly but not intimate relationships with her male coworkers. Her dealings with male colleagues generally didn't involve examining handmade erotic wood carvings over a spot of lunch. She had looked at Peter in surprise, but he was totally at ease, laughing at her unease.

The sculpture became famous as Sarah told their friends about it. She and Luke dined out on the story, even though Sarah was still the only one to have seen it. One day, she and Luke were around at Peter's place and there was the same carving on display.

'You forgot to mention one detail about the sculpture,' said Luke, laughing.

'What?'

'Where the man chose to put his penis.'

No wonder the woman looked so shocked.

*

But the work was cleverly done. Sarah overcame her consternation and asked Peter to carve a wooden plaque with the name of the house—*Cascina Cannella*. This was later cemented into the wall 'forever.'

The house becomes a companion, beloved. Each stone, carefully chipped and cleaned and replaced, invested with hope and a sense of belonging. *I have touched each of these stones. This house is my house and I will take care of it.*

CHAPTER 10 *bis*

Sarah has always struck a certain respectful awe into some members of the extended family—she is a stickler for doing things correctly, not taking short cuts, not skimping on the most appropriate materials to use in a project. It was through stories of Sarah's exploits that I embarked on plastering one of the bedrooms in our French house. When I say plastering, I mean very rough plastering, the kind that shows the trowel marks. I like it. It covers up the original coating of white paint I had mistakenly used on the grey stone walls in the spirit of brightening the room. This is not something Sarah would ever have done. She would have carefully cleaned each stone to display the different shades of grey—if you have ever tried to choose grey paint, you will know there are many, many shades, although possibly not a full fifty... It would have been beautiful.

Other stone walls have been left bare, after the white paint fiasco. Beams made of tree trunks, some still with their branches attached, straddle the roof and keep the stone gables at either end from caving in. Man-made wooden dowels attach beam to beam. The roof stays up as it has done for many, many years and the trustworthy stone walls are as solid in a raging thunderstorm as the oak tree trunk from which the central roof beam is made.

There is dust, but rural dust is not as sticky as urban dust. When spiders made their homes in the stone crevices, we realised we had conquered the damp that seeps into stone houses sitting on rain-soaked earth. Water no longer ran down the walls of the bedroom downstairs, pooling in the dimples and clefts and hollows of the stones and cooling the indoor air. We started with an inherited paraffin stove to warm the place up...

The first Christmas after we bought the house, we were celebrating around the kitchen table, cosy in the warmth of the paraffin heater that stood near the far end of the table, its metal skin almost glowing from the roaring fire inside. We could not yet use the fireplace as the previous inhabitants had crammed it with an old cooker that was fed with bottled gas and a defunct wood-burning stove. There was much work still to be done to prepare the chimney for a new wood-burning stove. We were therefore relying on the paraffin stove for winter heat.

The *Côtes de Rhône* was going down nicely. The children were tucked up in the next-door bedroom, the door kept slightly ajar by Grandpa's old slipper. Very cosy. But wait, the metal skin of the heater wasn't almost glowing, it *was* glowing, pulsating in fact. The steel tube that rose from the top of the stove and entered the chimney-breast was no longer steel grey, but glowing too, a translucent vermilion. As the realisation dawned that we might be having a chimney fire, we each stood up gingerly from the table, as if any movement might exacerbate the roaring of the flames, and tiptoed to the door. My dad opened the door, letting in the damp December air of the garden. My mum and I stepped out. My husband crept into the bedroom, woke the children, scooped up blankets and shooed them out into the garden. There, we lifted them into the ancient Land Rover, parked in the lee of the thick and sturdy and fire-proof stone wall of the back of the house, threw in the blankets, and breathed out slowly.

He didn't stop there though. Having rescued the children, he went in to rescue the wine. Of course. And so, as the stove did battle with the fire, we stood on the sopping wet grass in our slippers, clutching our wineglasses and thinking how to call the *sapeurs-pompiers*, the firefighters, without a phone. There was no one at home in the house nearest us. Should we wake up the neighbour in the nearby farmhouse? It would take a little while to reach. It was easy to see into our cottage as the double doors were made partly of old glass panes, which distorted—but did not hide —the interior. The door shutters had never been shut at all that evening in the customary way, as it had been too hot— that pulsating heat from the stove. As we continued to peer in from the safety of the cold, wet grass through the glass panes, bubbled and glitched with flaws, the stove piping started to look less red, its pulsing rhythm less intense. Had we got away with it? Did we dare go back inside?

We didn't want to admit it to ourselves, but we were quite shaken by the chimney fire episode. The next big project was the installing of a wood burning stove, an *insert*, to replace the paraffin heater. Slowly, little by little, the house was being transformed, taking on our characteristics, meeting our needs, reflecting who we were, or wanted to be.

CHAPTER 11
Pasta di nocciole or Hazelnut paste

Peter was back in Albania, finding a wife as it turned out. Cascina Cannella was still a building site. And il Cattivo had not gone away.

The hazelnuts scattered over the driveway as they fell from the old trees, still trying bravely to produce fruits. Hazelnuts have a distinctive taste. You could not mistake them for walnuts or pecans or brazil nuts or almonds. They are particularly delicious when crushed and made into a creamy paste. *Pasta di nocciole* spooned onto vanilla ice cream is heavenly. And so is hazelnut cake, *torta di nocciole*, one of Sarah's specialities. Sarah uses her own apricot jam, made with fruit from the garden.

Living next to a hazelnut grove should be heavenly too.

But for Sarah and Luke, it became the focus of all their anxiety.

Not long after they had made the big move to Piedmont, excited and nervous at starting anew, they made an offer to their neighbour, an offer to buy the hazelnut grove. It was an offer they continued to make over the years. But it was an offer he could refuse.

'*Non venderei mai la terra a voi per soldi, preferirei tenere la terra,*' (I would never sell land for money to you, I would rather keep the land,) he told them. And later, he emphasised the point with extreme relish. Shaking his hand into Luke's deliberately unreadable face, the fingers curled against the thumb to make a small hollow of rancour, he said again: '*Non vi venderei mai un centimetro della mia terra.*' (I would never sell *you* a *centimetre* of my land.)

Instead, the land became a dump for all his rubbish.

On one occasion, *il Cattivo's* son-in-law requested Sarah and Luke's cooperation regarding some work his family wanted to do on the disputed driveway. Sarah tried to strike a bargain: 'Of course. But first, could you move the rubbish behind the house?' The son-in-law expostulated: '*Le macerie, che macerie? I vostri rottami sono peggiori del nostri.*' (Rubbish, what rubbish? Your rubbish is worse than ours.) Sarah had leaned four planks of wood against the back of the house... *Il Cattivo* had back-up.

The hazelnut trees were, in fact, planted too close to the house and had grown way too high. When Sarah and Luke attached a copper pipe to the back of the house to allow the installation of a pellet stove—an environmentally friendly stove, fed by compressed wood pellets and with no noxious exhaust—*il Cattivo* accused them of not asking his permission to install the outlet pipe on their own back wall. He ranted about the dangers to the hazelnut trees. They would be set on fire—these sacred hazelnut trees that were planted too close and had grown too tall.

The trees continued to grow, unpruned, rarely tended, sometimes falling over onto the driveway in a high wind.

Piedmont, autumn 2007

Sarah noticed the hazelnuts rolling around on the driveway. She and Luke needed to take the car out. It ought not to be a problem. *Il Cattivo* was away, it seemed, and his sister was housesitting. Perhaps they should gather up the hazelnuts. It would be a shame to crush them all with the car. How on earth would that cause problems? Sarah went back into the house to fetch baskets and set about collecting them. It was a warm day in September, their fifth autumn here. As she picked them up—there were so many—she daydreamed about how they could use them. They certainly would store easily. Luke would have lots of ideas; he was such a creative cook. It was blissful, foraging under the deep blue September sky, hearing only the various buzzings and sighings of the insects in the grass, while *Basilico*, the cat with the bright blue eyes, curled around her ankles.

This was the last time Sarah was able to collect the fallen hazelnuts.

The sister, crouched in the house next door, had spied this business of collecting the nuts, she had evidently relayed the news to her brother. From then on, whenever a hazelnut hit the ground, he would make sure to chuck it back onto the grove. No one was going to have his hazelnuts.

There was a day when Luke and Sarah were preparing to take the car out to run some errands. The car was parked carefully in the driveway. There was only a slim strip of land where Luke could place the car without running the risk of complaints from *il Cattivo* about dangers to his buried water pipes, or to the slimy depths of his cesspit, or about the sunshine heating the metal roof of his car because all shady space was occupied. Luke had just got into the car, when Sarah remembered something she had left in the house. While Luke was waiting for her in the car, engine idling, he heard some scramblings and scufflings behind. What was going on? He looked in the driving mirror—nothing. He looked in his side mirror—my God, legs clothed in dark blue work pants, feet encased in thick leatherwork boots. Someone was kneeling behind the car. Luke got out to take a look... their neighbour, not a young man, stocky and not athletic, was on hands and knees, nose almost opposite the exhaust pipe, gathering the hazelnuts, breathing in the fumes, oblivious to Luke standing there, watching him, considering...

'My big moment and I missed it.' Luke laughs when he is recalling this incident—so many hazelnut incidents—'I could have put the car into reverse without realising...'

*

The driveway has sufficient room for cars to pass each other. You could see the whole dispute as Britain versus the European Union, a version of Brexit. On the one side rears the hard border of the massive stone wall of *il Cattivo's* house, while on the other the soft border of the strip of land that is home to the hazelnut trees. In this scenario, *Cattivo* becomes the Nigel Farage figure, desperate to take back control of borders, to rebuff efforts at compromise and to eject the foreigners. And Sarah and Luke are the soft border proponents, seeking only to maintain access to the space, not to control it, seeking a welcome in a foreign land, seeking tolerance.

Under Italian law, said *il Cattivo*, Sarah and Luke were not allowed to park their car in the driveway, because it interfered with his right to pass. Apparently, if you have direct passage across someone's land then you must make sure there is room to pass. The problem with this argument is that there is no real evidence to say the neighbour legally had the right to direct access to his house down Sarah and Luke's road. According to other locals in the neighbourhood with whom they were on solid, everyday, neighbourly, *normal* terms, it was simply an agreement between the two families who lived there before—the neighbouring house had access down *Cascina Cannella's* road and the previous inhabitants had access across *il Cattivo's* courtyard. But none of that really mattered when it came to the fact of Sarah and Luke moving in, not just as holiday people, but as real, long-term, staying-put neighbours. If they parked their cars there, then he, *il Cattivo*, was going to park his car there too. It was particularly important to park his car in the shade on sunny days, so he would park his car alongside theirs—this, despite the fact he had his own large courtyard and huge garage. It became a game, a tiresome, petty game. But it didn't feel like a game.

Gradually, the situation grew worse. The neighbour put up metal rods commonly used to reinforce concrete, each capped with a little *cappuccio* (hood), and connected them with red and white tape to delineate the soft border. This meant there wasn't sufficient room for another car to pass easily. Sarah and Luke's courtyard was full of rubble and building materials at that point. There was no place to park their cars, except on the winding mountain road. At one point, they had three delivery lorries parked on the road, full of building supplies. The two of them had to bring up all the building materials and equipment by wheelbarrow, around the hazelnut grove, up the driveway and into the courtyard. Sand was dumped on the driveway and then, quickly, Sarah and Luke had to wheelbarrow this around to the house. It could not be left where it had been delivered for even a moment, as that blocked the neighbour's way.

They still went on parking one or both of the cars in the driveway, but always on edge, waiting for the inevitable confrontation. It was extraordinarily frustrating. Luke was angry rather than intimidated. He is the son of a British Italian man who ran seafront businesses in the north of England—from video arcades to ice cream and doughnut joints. Fights would break out on a Saturday night in the arcade. Gino, and later on Luke's older brother Michael, were adept at chucking the drunks out. They weren't intimidated by the fists and belligerence. (Knives are a modern phenomenon. Michael often says regretfully in his soft Lancashire accent, 'what happened to just hitting each other? Now they have to stab each other to death?') Luke has been protected from this to some extent, the educated one who went to university, sought a professional living away from the rough end of town. He retains, however, the core Rinaldi belief in defending what is yours. He tempers the intense irritation *il Cattivo* provokes in him because of Sarah and the effects of this strange and unlooked-for hostility on her. But they couldn't stay out of his way all the time and Luke was as determined as any of his Italian neighbours that he wasn't going to be driven from his land.

One night, they were heading out for a party and as Luke was reversing the car down the driveway—it was extremely tight—the wing mirror of the car hit one of the metal posts, bending it and knocking off one of the *cappucci*. The damage was slight, the post barely deviated from the straight and narrow, but it was noticeable.

'It's only a sodding metal post,' Luke muttered to himself. '*Che peccato*'—too bad.

They forgot about the mishap and had a great evening with their tall Norwegian friends, Per with the ginger beard and Marianne with the long chestnut hair, always caught up in a glittery metal clip. They were a couple of similar age and circumstances, if not of height, who had the same depth of attachment to their life in Italy. They ran a smallholding a few kilometres from *Cascina Cannella*, higher up the hill, and reached via many bends in the steep winding road. They loved Luke and Sarah's *Cattivo* stories but were aghast, and sometimes not always convinced of the full truth of them. Luke tried to make them funny, while Sarah did not want to reveal how severely she was affected. It did not fit with the story they wove for themselves of their own lives here in this enchanted place.

They returned home late, forgetting about the damaged metal post, the lost *cappuccio*.

Lean though he is, Luke has haunches like steel hawsers. This is because he is addicted to a daily circuit on his bike around the mountainside whenever he is home. On the morning following the bending of the post incident, one of those blissful spring days, sunshine yellow against a blue backdrop, not yet too hot, Luke saddled up the bike, set off joyfully and did the usual round of his favourite spots. First, he sailed past the Rossis' farm where the dogs hailed him in a crescendo of delighted barks. Then he made his regular stop at the farm of an ancient couple who kept their dog chained in an old stone outhouse with a view over the dirt yard where grass refused to grow.

Luke had deployed his extraordinary ability to persuade. He had almost taken a step backwards when he met the old farmer's wife for the first time, for the asymmetry of her features gave her the grotesque aspect of a lopsided brown gnome. As he cajoled her into letting him take the unfortunate dog for a stroll sometimes, she allowed herself a transformative smile that lent charm to her unfortunate face. This morning, there was no sign of the gnome woman. He dismounted, leaned the bike against the outside of the stone shelter and clicked his tongue softly. The dog waddled out to greet him, his short thick tail wagging as fast as possible, given its girth. Luke had named him *Formaggio*, which sounds better in Italian than Cheese. The dog was short-legged, with a bristly sand-coloured coat. He had the look of an overweight corgi surprised to find himself so fat. Luke slipped a homemade collar and lead, fashioned from rope, around his neck, and the two set off on their customary outing. Luke had found out that if he slipped the rope collar off the dog's neck and offered him his freedom, *Formaggio* would turn tail and head briskly back to his kennel. Luke always found this oddly perturbing, but gave up trying to instil some rebellion into the dog. Old habits die hard indeed.

It was around midday. The sun was high in the sky. All across the valley, the trees and vines stretched out to shake off the chill of winter, nervously growing green-tipped foliage to clothe their bony branches. On his return, free-wheeling down the road, innocent, carefree, happy to be home after days on the road, Luke was greeted by an angry man with a metal post in his hand. *Il Cattivo* was brandishing the bent pole, waiting for Luke. It was scramble time. He ditched the bike, ran to the house.

'Sarah, get the video camera. Quick. He's going nuts out there. He's threatening to hit me with that wretched post.' (Get the evidence; prove your case. Luke had not forgotten this lesson from the previous encounter with the police.)

Luke was fully prepared to go back, even provoke *Cattivo* to hit him, just to nail the bastard on camera. He

149

knew this would be a way to get him to boil over, 'touching his bloody plastic *cappuci*.' But did he really want to be hit over the head with a metal post?

'I wasn't wearing my helmet,' he recalls later. 'It would have been useful.' He laughs, but his laughter is unsmiling.

'I can't have someone assaulting me.' Luke was enraged. Sarah took control. She couldn't get the video recorder to work; the damn thing had seized up. But she did have the tape recorder.

They rang the police... not for the first time.

'*Apprezziamo la sua telefonata. Per piacere richiamare dopo pranzo,*' (We appreciate your call. Please call back after lunch,) said the machine...

By the time they called back, there had been a development.

'*C'è un problema. Dovete venire alla stazione di polizia.*' (There's a problem, you need to come in to the police station.)

In the two hours of lunchtime that they waited before calling back, the neighbour had filed a complaint against *them*.

'*Gli ha sputato addosso,*' (You spat on him,) said the laconic voice on the other end of the line.

Luke was beside himself.

'Well, you did spit,' said Sarah, earnestly.

'I spat on the ground,' said Luke, indignantly. 'I couldn't think of any words, so I just spat on the ground in front of him.' Luke imitated spitting at *il Cattivo's* feet. 'And that was enough in his simple mind to think "I'm in trouble here, I'm going to pre-empt trouble by saying *he* spat on *me.*"' Luke was furious.

They went to the police, not to lodge a complaint against the neighbour, but to defend themselves against him. They were the ones in trouble.

The local *caserma* (police station), an austere building of concrete blocks, was surrounded by a high fence topped with barbed wire. They had to press the buzzer at the locked gate to gain entrance.

Il Cattivo was already there—and so, to their surprise, was his wife. They were each seated on plastic chairs that barely contained their behinds, facing a large, shiny desk. They looked straight in front of them, not even a twitch in the direction of Sarah and Luke. Inside the building, it felt hotter than outside. The pondweed green of the walls made Sarah feel as if she were underwater. She was dreading the confrontation, sick with anticipation. Apparently, the neighbours had already given their version of the incident to the police. It was up to Sarah and Luke to refute something they hadn't heard.

The *Commissario*, the same man who had adjudicated once in their favour about *il Cattivo's* dogs, was sitting behind the desk. In front of him lay an open dossier. Shuffling could be heard somewhere in the building. Where were they coming from? For one weird moment, Sarah imagined herself in a film. Wartime. She's in black and white. Someone is being tortured in the next room. It was an effort to bring herself back into colour.

The *Commissario* pushed a large hand through his thick black hair, streaked with iron grey. His hand resembled a spider with heavy legs, so furred were the fingers with black hairs.

'*Okay, mostrami cos' hai.*' (Okay, show me what you have.) He gestured to Luke to give him the tape recording.

'*Non hanno niente, non hanno niente, lo dicono solo.*' (They haven't got anything, they haven't got anything, they're just saying it.) *Il Cattivo* kept repeating this, thrusting his hands forward for emphasis, addressing himself only to the *Commissario*. *Signora* Cattivo, meanwhile, her voice fluttering, continued to repeat '*Vivo qui da trent'anni, Maresciallo.*' (I've been living here for thirty years, Officer.)

It was as if Luke and Sarah were not there. The *Cattivi* had banished them from the story.

Luke held out his hand to Sarah for the tape. She fumbled in her basket, but it wasn't there. The more she fumbled, the more *Cattivo* kept on with his refrain: *'non hanno niente, non hanno niente, lo dicono solo.'*

Sarah—the strong, independent Sarah who had been a successful project manager, who had travelled Europe on her own, who inspired a certain awe among her own family and friends—started to cry.

'Oh, piange sempre,' (Oh, she's always crying,) said *il Cattivo*, dismissing the tears. He and his wife sat impassively, as Sarah dried her eyes with her thumbs. She didn't want to go on fumbling in the basket. She knew she had tossed the tape in there as they left for the police station. She *knew* she had. Everything was conspiring against them. Even inanimate objects were ganging up. She just wanted to be at home, among her plants and vegetable garden, talking to the cats and thinking about the building work, about where to locate the balconies to replace the hayloft (not one, but *three* balconies), and about dinner tonight and about… oh, anything that didn't concern wretched *Cattivo* and his wretched wife with her hairsprayed curls and fleshy bottom pushing against her white trousers.

'Here—here it is.' Luke lifted the tape triumphantly from the bottom of the basket where it had lain under a bundle of rosemary wrapped in newspaper. He handed it to the *Commissario* who was gazing, judge-like, upon the proceedings, his furry hands spread across the dossier. He stood and walked out from behind the desk, not a tall man but an imposing one with his broad shoulders and the sharpness of his pressed uniform

On the tape:

Cattivo: *'Ti farò la testa come un pallone.'* (I'm going to make your head like a balloon.) He was saying this while brandishing the metal pole at Luke.

The *Commissario* listened. Then he pronounced: *'Avete quattro cani, sei gatti e dieci persone in quel villaggio e non potevate vivere insieme. Dovete cominciare a imparare a vivere insieme.'* (You've got four dogs, six cats and ten people in that village and you couldn't live together. You're gonna *have* to start learning to live together.)

*

Sarah and Luke came to know the local police quite well, enough to feel a certain unease when the current *Commissario* moved on. Little of a concrete nature might be done, but Sarah felt that he at least had some sympathy with their predicament.

Sarah was forced to file another statement after the grass-cutting affair.

Cascina Cannella was a demanding place, with essential needs that could not be ignored. Even now, there is much to do in order to maintain the land: caring for the vines, tending the vegetables, looking after the garden, mowing the grass… Back in the days when Sarah and Luke were engulfed in building work, renovations and finding their way around their promised land, this work of upkeep still had to be done alongside the major projects.

Sarah is in the habit of keeping the grass down using a strimmer—it is the only piece of equipment that can be wielded easily to deal with the grass growing towards the back of the house and along the strips that divide the vines. Most of the land is planted up. Even so, the grass that remains needs maintenance. This was also the case, during the building work.

Sarah usually wears ear defenders when she uses the strimmer. She was cutting the grass not long after that somewhat dispiriting visit to the police station, happily isolated from the world, concentrating hard on the job. Suddenly, she felt a thump between her shoulder blades. She almost lost her balance.

'*Questo è il mio pezzo di terra. Cosa stai facendo nel mio pezzo?*' (That's my piece of grass. What are you doing, cutting my piece of grass?)

Sarah swung round to face *il Cattivo*. He was thrusting his hefty chin at her, greasy and lightly stubbled in grey. This wasn't the first time he had crept up on her while she was wearing her earphones, working on the land. She would be strimming in the vineyard and he would appear, waving his hand in her face, strimming in her path, forcing her to stop, both wordless with fury.

This time, however, it went beyond intimidation. This time, *il Cattivo* laid his hand on her.

And this time, the police came to interview them at the house.

There was disbelief when Sarah pointed out to the two officers the small piece of grass that was at the centre of the controversy. Exclamations, hand gestures, the shaking of heads from the pair, one tall, one shorter, both incredulous. They went next door to talk to *il Cattivo*. Then… silence.

'We never heard any more about it. They don't want trouble like that, they say it's not up to them to resolve it,' explains Luke. He draws his shoulders round his ears, holds out his hands, palms facing upwards. I almost expect him to say, like an American gangster, 'what you gonna do, huh?' He doesn't. But it is clear they have both become resigned.

'They say: "We don't have the jurisdiction to resolve this, you lot need to get together." Proving these things, that's always the problem.'

'They didn't believe us anyway, they said it takes two sides,' says Sarah.

'Well, no-one wants to get involved, really. No-one wants to take sides,' Daisy chimes in, but this does not go down too well.

'Even some of our friends thought we were making it up.' Sarah looks to Luke for corroboration. 'Nobody understands,' she adds, sadly.

There is a pause, while we sit in thoughtful silence in the quiet garden, looking over the valley. We are all peaceful now.

'He always waves to me.' Luke is disdainful. 'It's easy to wave to someone…'

'Even now, when the vineyard is looked after by someone else, he goes out and strims the line between our land and his,' says Sarah, animated again. And she adds, 'He's completely mad. He's like a dog, marking his own borders. That's what he does. Every border has to be controlled.'

Ah, the man for Brexit.

CHAPTER 11 *bis*

Sarah's version of hazelnut cake, or *torta di nocciole*, is like a Bakewell tart, using hazelnuts instead of almonds. It is pastry-based, with a thin layer of home-made apricot jam that has been cooked, making it very concentrated. The layer of short-crust pastry is spread with the concentrated jam, then topped with a light hazelnut cake. Sarah doesn't remember at first where she found the cake recipe, probably rummaging around among some old cookbooks.

CHAPTER 12
Peter is back

Piedmont, spring 2007

Vast piles of stone and concrete and chipped off pieces of plaster; dirt always under your feet, scuffed up continually; the air thick with dust, it's in your eyelashes and teeth and on your tongue; the sheer volume of debris so that you can't move without tripping up on a chunk of ragged stone; the sounds of chipping, plastering, heaving, of men grunting and swearing and yelling; the heat and the brilliant light and the lines of sweat tickling down your body; it felt like the building work would never end. Sarah got up every morning, her mind fixed on the next job, her thoughts concerned only with the strength of materials, the mechanics of construction. While Luke had to leave home each week, his world stretching out across the highways of Europe as he sought customers, Sarah was leaving her warm morning bed to travel the short length to the building site, her world narrowing to this scene of detritus and destruction and debris outside her back door. Her tired, over-worked body awoke with renewed enthusiasm—early, very early. She beat the building team in getting out of bed, preparing for the day and laying her hands on those stones.

*

The finance police arrived as the builders were preparing to resume work on the construction of the carport, adjacent to the erstwhile hayloft, now a self-contained apartment (the one where we do much of our talking and to which I have become attached). The builders, who were as usual Macedonians, were watching with bemusement as Luke hung out the washing in the courtyard. He was dressed for work in a fresh candy-striped linen shirt tucked in to pressed khakis, a light cotton scarf looped about his neck —the sort of smart casual outfit you would expect on a European man going to work, but that would put a certain type of Englishman right off his cornflakes. Sarah had already been up for hours and was taking a break, perched on one of the stone steps that descend the outside wall from the balcony of the upstairs apartment. She was tying the lace on one of her workman's boots, her face hidden by the large floppy hat that kept most of her in the shade. The builders were looking from one to the other.

'They probably think I'm a slacker,' said Luke, glancing over at Sarah. She grinned across at him. She didn't mind being something of a star. All that mattered to her was getting on with the building work. Sometimes Sarah thought that it would never end. Neither she nor Luke spoke of these feelings to the other. They did not want to admit to such thoughts. It would have felt like the betrayal of a commitment, the breaking of a vow. (Daisy remembers Luke confiding to her quietly, out of Sarah's earshot, 'I'm just looking forward to not always having work to do, Mum.')

The visit from the finance police was unexpected, but not completely surprising. The *Guardia di Finanza* is part of the Italian police system, responsible for dealing with tax evasion, detecting money laundering and guarding Italy's waters.

There were two of them, men of a certain age whose worn features betrayed no emotion. They were, however, insistent on speaking to Luke and Sarah. This was not going to be quick. Luke's heart sank as he invited them to sit at the kitchen table. What on earth could this be about? Surely they had put behind them all that trouble about the disputed payments from a couple of years ago? Luke fussed around the kitchen, offering coffee (*'no grazie'*), moving chairs, refolding tea towels. Eventually, Sarah also came into the kitchen to join them, having changed out of her work gear and into a dress (she only wore a dress when she was going to the market or into one of the larger towns or if they had been invited out for a special evening). She was also wearing red lipstick and had brushed her hair so that it shone. The men sat impassively, exuding no air of friendliness, and unusually, failing to fall for Sarah's charm. They had their folders in front of them. One of the men, the one with a fabulously Roman nose, opened the conversation. It seemed Luke and Sarah owed back taxes on work carried out by a builder they had employed some time ago.

Peter.

Before Sarah could catch enough breath to exclaim how this was all rubbish (*tutte sciocchezze*), the man without the Roman nose (his was more bulbous and slightly pock-marked) looked out of the window, his attention caught by movement outside.

'*Chi sono?*' (Who are they?) he asked, nodding at the builders.

Luke tensed. He explained that the builders were working for a company carrying out work for them, desperately trying to put some distance between them and the Macedonians; he had a nervous feeling about what might be coming next.

'*Sono in regola?*' (Are they legal?) the Roman nose man asked. He pushed himself back in his chair, scraping the painstakingly restored floor tiles. Sarah winced.

'*Vado a parlargli.*' (I'm going to speak to them.) And off they went.

Luke was beside himself. It was frustrating enough that the police had come to deliver the unexpected bad news about Peter, but it looked as if they had also come searching for more. And found it.

He and Sarah exchanged glances, knowing what the other was thinking. Were they legal? Luke had no idea. He just knew that if they weren't, they were all going to be in trouble. It was their responsibility to know if all of the employees on their work site were legal, as well as the employees' own responsibility to be aware of their legal status.

Fortunately, this time, they *were* legal. (The Italian authorities tend to take a harsh line on illegal immigrants, but most Italians would rather help out an individual immigrant than report them to the police.) Sarah and Luke breathed again... but not for long.

*

Peter had come back from Albania with his new wife and, it seemed, the expectation that he would continue working on the house, something that couldn't happen for a range of reasons. Sarah and Luke had employed a team of builders with different skills to convert the old hayloft into two apartments, with a view to making money in the future from offering bed and breakfast on an informal, friends-of-friends basis. This work was much more about construction, about sheer grinding hard physical work, than aesthetics and beauty. Peter's talents, so appreciated by Sarah, would not be suited.

A long-running and tangled dispute was set in motion.

One morning, Peter arrived at the worksite, with the intention of joining the other builders, in spite of all their discussions. He climbed onto the scaffolding, making as if to join the team. As usual, Sarah was up there too, working alongside them. It was an amicable arrangement, each builder concentrating on their particular area of construction.

Peter's arrival disrupted the peace. Sarah had to deal with the situation, but felt ill-equipped to argue with Peter. The scaffolding was reasonably sturdy, but nevertheless, only as stable as steel pipes and planks of wood can be. Peter was becoming more and more disturbed, the bones of his face rigid with anger. He grabbed Sarah's arms and pushed her, causing her to lose her footing. She fell from the scaffolding. It wasn't a steep drop; the scaffolding wasn't that high. No one knew what to do, how to react. The air stood still with the shock of it.

This was Peter, Sarah's fellow creator, the man whose ability as a stonemason was responsible partly for the beauty of the house. When he pushed her, some part of Sarah became frightened, in spite of herself. It was so unbelievable.

She asked him to leave. He wouldn't. Instead, he continued to work, alongside the other builders—who did not want to get involved.

Sarah had nothing left to fight him with. Luke was far away. When the usual rules of behaviour from your own culture fail to apply in your adopted culture, what are you supposed to do? You are both powerless and furious—and sometimes, frightened. Sarah went into the kitchen, sat on the windowsill, shook.

Peter decided eventually to leave, perhaps realising he had made a serious mistake. Two days later, he returned, apparently with the intention of working, as if nothing untoward had occurred. Again, Sarah said no, this was not going to happen. Go. *Vada*

Yet Peter returned, this time accompanied by several other men. Luke was home this time. Both he and Sarah were genuinely disturbed. Were Peter and his henchmen intending to beat them up? This did not happen. It was machismo in action. Only machismo, but enough to make Sarah and Luke believe there could be repercussions. More uninvited visits, perhaps damage to their house, perhaps worse… Luke usually dismissed this kind of absurdly exaggerated masculine behaviour; he was exposed to it often in his travels around Europe, but always deflected it with a joke, an ironic aside, a shrug and a gesture.

This was different, personal. It was threatening Sarah, making her unhappy. Luke felt it deeply. 'They could have beaten us to smithereens.'

'That lived with us for a long time,' Sarah says, 'you never knew if he would do something…'

Peter got the message, left them alone, finally. But he continued to pursue them with various claims, via different solicitors' letters. He tried to take them to court twice, the first time involved a bill that Peter claimed had not been paid—something Sarah and Luke denied. They found themselves a lawyer and letters went back and forth for months. Peter unearthed 'witnesses' in a neighbouring village, whom Sarah and Luke had never met, even though they claimed to have been at *Cascina Cannella*. 'Complete liars,' according to Sarah. Ultimately, the suit was dropped just before they were supposed to go to court. The story kept changing.

Peter was ordered to pay Luke and Sarah's costs, which had mounted up quickly, running into several thousands of euros. Peter protested that he was penniless—aside, that is, from the garage full of valuable antique cars. Somehow, he found the sum—when he was threatened with the loss of one of his beloved cars. And apart from the occasional bouncing payment, the debt was settled. All was calm. It was over. Or so they thought…

A few months later… another letter from another solicitor. This time, they were accused of not having paid sufficient taxes on Peter's wages. The charge was spurious, and provably spurious. It was eventually dropped, but not without taking its toll on them. 'There was always this'– Sarah puts her hand to her throat, makes a low growling noise—'this *ansia (*anxiety).'

At the heart of it all, perhaps jealousy lay. Peter and Sarah had created their own intense world, but it could not possibly last. Perhaps Peter was trying to recreate it, to prolong something that had been so pleasurable and satisfying.

Whatever the cause, that world was now in the past. Peter had, finally, to accept it.

*

For Sarah, it was like a betrayal. For a time, she couldn't bear to run across him in the nearby town, or on one or other of her errands. And yet, she loved it; she loved the building and the camaraderie. Peter's behaviour taught her to distance herself, to check her emotions. When it came time to convert the hayloft, Sarah was in control. The man who broke one of the expensive drainage sections was not allowed near them again. 'Look, I don't want him doing that work anymore. They cost 50 euros each and I'm not paying for that broken one'—all this in their shared language, builders' Italian. Sarah heard the other builders whispering in shock at her fierceness. When a crane had to be used to deliver the vast, solid beams, Sarah sat on the beams to guide them, swinging across the building site, majestic.

'We were so lucky with so many things. There was so much that could have gone wrong, really badly wrong.' Specific height regulations on rooms meant the sandy scrap of land that became the courtyard, now resplendent in its cobbles and rose-pink terracotta pots, had to be dug out to allow the kitchen floor to be lowered to the correct level.

When the builders were excavating some of the land around the hayloft, they came across an old well sealed in concrete. It had been used as a rubbish pit. It would have to be investigated. 'Normally, you send something down to test if there's oxygen.' Sarah is succinct: 'If there's no oxygen, you're dead.' There was oxygen. They know this because, impatient, the builders tied two ladders together *'with a bit of old rope,'* stuck them into the well and climbed down to take a look.

The work on the hayloft conversion took about eighteen months. Builders were being paid by the hour, which was a mistake, in hindsight. Sarah felt she had to be vigilant, like an old-fashioned mill owner, constantly on guard for slackers. Working with Peter, just the two of them, seekers after the same perfection, was very different, more rewarding, despite the souring of their relationship.

Il Cattivo even allowed the delivery truck with sections of balcony to cross his courtyard because there was no other way to gain access. Were relations becoming warmer? No.

CHAPTER 12 *bis*

Piedmont, the present

Time stops.

The photographs show you fragments of how this Italian life has been built; you can't smell the dust in the air or taste the cement particles on your tongue; you can't hear the relentless noisiness of the machines. We are looking at pictures of the old hayloft this fine and beautiful morning from the luxury of the future, with all work completed. Sarah and Luke have spent a long time reaching this happy stage. They appreciate their surroundings, can hardly believe this is how they live.

As we look at the elegant length of the converted hayloft, Daisy catches our thoughts, 'do you remember when we all descended on you that summer, your first year here?' We smile—the four of us. I am opposite Daisy at the stone table on the edge of the garden. Sarah is sitting in front of a pile of photo albums, with Luke hovering, read to serve us coffee and whatever our hearts desire.

We are back in the summer of 2003, sitting around the long wooden 'table' in the old hayloft. Sarah has created table from a door she found abandoned about the pl and she has covered it with a red and white chec tablecloth (of course) and posies of lavender and roser tied with ribbon. The detritus of a rural family hou around us—rabbit hutches, lichen-covered terracotta tiles, slightly moth-eaten baskets with wooden slats a base, in which sat the green glass demijohns used to the wine. Sarah and Luke have stacked the hutche the demijohn baskets, carefully stored the tiles aga stone walls (one or two are on the table, transforr bread baskets) and the hayloft now has the air of restaurant. Luke stands in front of the cooker at c

the building, apron wrapped around him, whipping up delicious things, while we drink our wine and chatter and wonder at this place. Beneath our feet is a soil floor, dry and dusty, wisps of straw tickling our toes; above, rackety wooden beams hold up (we hope) the floor of the hayloft.

It is Sarah and Luke's first full year of living in the house. We are the extended family, not so much invited as desperately curious and determined not to be left out of any party. In the silence that follows our reminiscences and laughter, we think of those beloved people who witnessed the start of this grand adventure, but who have not lived to see its magnificent outcome.

This scene of us sitting in the old hayloft, happy in that moment, is a picture that we carry in our collective imagination. In a way, this house has become a gathering-place for friends and family, not just a home. It is a gift to us all, as it must have been to the previous families who lived here. It holds our remembered happiness as well as our happiness now.

CHAPTER 13
Wine and renovations

Piedmont, the present

'Oh piss off.'

Daisy, Luke's mother, has had enough. She gets up from the table where she is eating breakfast to look over the balcony rail from where the persistent buzzing is emanating.

Il Cattivo is strimming the corner of the hazelnut grove, the corner that happens to be beneath the balcony and just off to its side. The buzzing is underpinned by a whine that speeds up or slows down, according to which patch of dirt in the hazelnut grove is currently under attack. The buzzing and whining have provided the background to the conversation since we all—Luke, Daisy, Sarah and I—sat down to breakfast.

'He's got a nice cloud of dust around him.' Daisy laughs.

'Hope it gets into his lungs,' says Sarah.

We all laugh, except Sarah.

We're sitting on the balcony that belongs to one of the two self-contained apartments attached to the main house, but extended out from it at a right angle—the former hayloft.

The balcony is built over the bedroom of the apartment below and is open on three sides. Luke and Sarah have stacked a substantial log pile against the rail that faces onto the hazelnut grove and topped it with woven baskets and decorative objects, but still the buzz of the strimmer is undimmed.

There is a large pine tree that rears up, up and away on the side that looks out over their vineyard and across the valley, fragmenting the vista and turning it into snapshots through its feathery branches.

The apartments enable Luke and Sarah to make a small living from *Cascina Cannella*. They rent them occasionally, mainly to friends. Luke is making plans to stop working for the food ingredients company that employs him and where he finds himself having to schmooze with customers he doesn't much like. He is amiable, soft-spoken, but with a knife-sharp sense of where the bullshit is located. Right now, the travelling three days a week is becoming a burden. He wants to devote himself full time to working with Sarah, caring for their land and cultivating the vineyard. The finances have to be in place.

The strimming continues, only louder. Sarah is trying to ignore the racket and to placate her mother in law.

'Not that big a patch, is it?' Daisy says loudly, laughing. She is generally soft-spoken. Her laughter does not hide her irritation.

Sarah soldiers on, talking about the first time they took charge of making their wine from their own small vineyard. In the beginning, they were happy to continue the arrangement with the local farmer, *Signor* Rossi who was tending their vines as well as his own and selling their combined harvest of grapes to the local cooperative. Sarah and Luke's attention was mainly taken by the building work; they had little energy left over to worry too much about the vineyard. Their neighbourly arrangement with the Rossi family suited everyone. However, they decided to have a go at winemaking as *Signor* Rossi had enough grapes to fill the designated quota from his own vineyard that year.

'If you have more than your quota, you don't get any money for the extra grapes,' explains Sarah.

She and Luke didn't want to waste their grapes so they borrowed a *torchio*, a winepress small enough to fit on the back of a truck, which they used to make their strong sweet wine, *Moscato passito*.

168

'We crushed the grapes here in the little machine and made the wine in the green demijohns with the help of a local producer who told us what chemicals to add.'

'The yeasts…' Luke interjects.

'Then we put it in our kitchen, next to the fire because it has to be warm, it can't be too cold, and it sat there all year, all winter, bubbling slowly and we'd take samples to see what the sugar to alcohol ratio was, and then when it was ready, we filtered it.'

The last time they made wine themselves was in 2009.

'We put the 2009 wine in front of the fire so that the fermentation would start. It didn't. It went extremely slowly, which meant it remained extremely sweet and didn't have the preservation properties of the alcohol so it kept getting a little bit of a film on the top,' remembers Luke.

The problem was that the quantities were so minute and they didn't have the proper equipment, so he overestimated the metabisulphite (a preserving agent) and that stopped the fermentation.

'The only way to kick start it naturally was to wait another year and add the *must* (freshly pressed fruit juice, usually grape juice, that contains the skins, seeds and stems) from the next year and in the end, it worked,' says Luke. He is at ease with winemaking processes and terms. Italian wine is his passion. And his favourite place in the world is his temperature-controlled, purpose-built wine cellar, next to the kitchen and entered upon invitation only.

Tales of winemaking have distracted us from the activities of *il Cattivo* for a brief while, but then the strimming starts again, insistent.

Daisy says: 'This is very upsetting because there's nothing there. Just soil.'

Sarah says: 'The Macedonians—the builders—said if we wanted to get rid of him, they knew a way. We only had to say the word.'

There is a brief silence. A while ago, Sarah and Luke's Macedonian builders were working for him, for *il Cattivo*, explains Sarah.

'We used to wave to them. And then one day, one of them called me over to see what they were doing. Once they'd finished, they came here for a drink. They said he was the worst person they'd ever had to work for—because he'd stand over them, looking at what they were doing and saying nothing. He was just there.'

'And you think they meant it?' asks Daisy.

'Oh yeah.'

We laugh. We want to shout *'bastardo'* at *il Cattivo*. All together, in unison. Him and his sodding strimmer.

But we don't. Sarah won't let us. If we show him that he has got under our skins, he will be pleased.

'He will have won,' says Sarah. And she's not going to let him win. Whatever it costs her. She has spent too much time building her defences, digging herself into her life here.

*

When Sarah and Luke first moved to *Cascina Cannella*, the thought of the vineyard was exhilarating—their own vineyard—but it was also daunting; how on earth do you *cultivate* a vineyard? They were happy to continue the arrangement with *Signor* Rossi. However, at a certain point, the contract expired, and the arrangement continued on a more *ad hoc* basis. Sarah and Luke (but mainly Sarah) took over the tending of the vines. By now, the vineyard was half its original size, a portion of the land having been made over to another use, and consequently a more manageable proposition for Sarah working on her own. She had picked up relevant pruning knowledge from watching others at work and helping in neighbouring vineyards. Now she was ready to put that experience into the service of their land.

(There is little Sarah will not tackle. She watches others, learns, practises, conquers. Where necessary, she signs up for a professionally taught course, such as dry stone walling. She has built all the dry stone walls that criss-cross the garden.)

They started to work the vineyard, but soon realised they were paying for vine treatments each year yet were not making any money from the grapes. Naturally, there was nothing for it but to take over the treatments themselves.

There are no picturesque scenes of Sarah, in trailing pale linen and a straw hat, languidly snipping at her vines. Instead, over her baggy t-shirt smeared with dirt, she wears a small pump-action backpack containing fungicide to spray the vines for pests and diseases. The tank needs to be filled seven times each spraying session. She and Luke take it in turns to trudge through the vines with the backpack strapped to their backs, sweating wildly under protective gloves and hats. It is impossible to use a small tractor, as other vine growers do, because the land is too steep and the strips between the rows too narrow. It must all be done by hand.

This artisan approach to spraying suits Sarah and Luke. 'Vineyards look beautiful,' says Sarah, 'but think of the chemicals that are applied—potent insecticides twice a year, fungicides every seven to ten days. You don't want to buy a house with a vineyard very close by—the powerful machinery that farmers use now sends the spray a long way.' She thinks that *Cascina Cannella* is safe from this alien spray, despite being surrounded by vineyards, because it is positioned sufficiently far away.

'We don't get anybody else's spray, only our own,' she says, adding with satisfaction, 'and we now have control over that.'

Romantic notions of tending your own vineyard under an Italian sun were soon buried, like Sarah herself, under a heap of heavy-weight experience. The land demands much of its human caretakers in return for its usefulness. There are no short cuts. Very little money had been spent on the vineyard at *Cascina Cannella*, while the earth had been saturated with weed killer.

'It was a mess,' says Sarah.

Old posts had to be replaced. But of course, they were anchored in cement boots. The string that was used as scaffolding for the vines—a common means of support because of its cheapness—had to be replaced with wire. The ground had to be raked into submission and the vegetation beaten back with a strimmer. Sarah eventually succeeded in turning the area into a wildflower haven.

'It's a lot of work to keep it trimmed, but so beautiful and so much healthier for the environment.' Sarah never rests.

They continued to make the *passito* wine for their own consumption, but as Luke says 'there's only so much sweet wine you can drink.' They tried selling their surplus grapes on the black market, but the returns were small. Ultimately, they asked the farmer to relinquish his rights to sell the grapes, to which he agreed. In a small local restaurant one day, Sarah fell into conversation with the owners, a mother and daughter team—strong and wiry women with black shiny hair—forced into their roles through tragedy, the death of the husband or father in an accident at work. Sitting at one of the tables on the terrace, warmth seeping into their skin, they agreed an arrangement. The mother and daughter partnership would pay upkeep costs on the vineyard and buy the grapes, both the Moscato grapes, picked first, and the second-harvest grapes, which are left in fruit trays to dry under Sarah and Luke's car-port roof. Sarah and Luke would tend the vineyard and deliver the grapes.

'How much of your time does the vineyard take up these days?' I ask.

They will not get rich from this venture. 'I see it as a glorified hobby that makes some money,' proclaims Sarah, happily. And while they no longer make any wine, this 'hobby' involves:

Vineyard work—grass cutting and maintenance: two hours every fortnight;

Pruning—one full day;

Maintenance—regular;

Removing old vines—one full day;

Planting new vines—one full day;

Adding nutrients to the earth—one hour here and there;

Tying down the vines—one full day (they no longer use metal ties to fasten the vines; instead, they use willow strips. This entails first making the willow strips…);

Taking off old vine branches and shredding them for use in the garden to suppress weeds (nothing is wasted)—two hours every week from May to August;

Spraying—two hours every ten to twelve days;

Picking and delivery—one day for the Moscato grapes, one day for the passito late grapes.

In addition, they collect two tractor loads of vine cuttings to shred, apart from their own, to be used in the garden…

A serious hobby, indeed.

During one recent visit, Daisy and I join them in the late harvest, walking up and down the rows, basket between us, bending and picking, picking and bending. It is early in the morning. The usual breakfast of summer cake, yogurt and home grown fruit (today is pomegranate day—pink seedy pulp staining the cake and the yogurt)—was hours ago and we have been marshalled for work.

This is not an unpleasant way to spend a morning. After a couple of hours, we think we have finished. We stand up straight (bliss) and survey our results. Tray upon tray of small, almost shrivelled, brownish-gold grapes are displayed on the courtyard stones, drying in the sun. They will soon be ready for loading into the van and delivery to the winemaker.

Good work.

*

Sarah could not believe she had signed up for this. She rolled over onto her side to heave her aching body from the bed in the early morning of what was going to become a brutally hot day. Seated on the edge of the bed, she ruefully examined the bruises on both thighs from having been poked repeatedly by the stiff dark stems of the vines yesterday during the ten hours of intense grape picking. It was the first day of the harvest at their neighbours' farmhouse, a couple of kilometres down the road from *Cascina Cannella*. Sarah was already regretting her offer of help.

Still, no time for that now. She had promised. Giovanni and Rosa would be expecting her, as would their large and unprepossessing son. Luke was already on the road. He would not be home for days. Standing in the cool of the kitchen, preparing breakfast—more than her usual yogurt and cake, she needed the ballast of bread and butter— Sarah asked herself out loud, not for the first time, why she was doing this.

She knew, of course. The old couple, in their late seventies, but who looked older and more used up by life than you might expect, had saved her. Oh, it was not as dramatic as that, perhaps, but it felt as if it were. Plagued by *il Cattivo's* persistent surveillance of their shared driveway that ran along the edge of the hazelnut grove, Sarah had decided not to engage with the enemy. The builders were using their courtyard as storage for building materials, debris and general supplies, while Luke parked his company

174

car on the side of the mountain road, as visibly as possible. (You never knew what would be coming round the bend next.) There was no room for Sarah's car. And she wasn't going to use that driveway and face *il Cattivo's* angry complaining. Nor did she want to face his two aggressive dogs, barking and spitting at her. Giovanni and Rosa had offered her a way out—she could park on their land. This arrangement lasted for two or three years...

Two or three years!

When she recounts the story years later, Daisy and I are stunned—even though Daisy has heard this before. It just hadn't sunk in—the sheer tedium of it, leaving aside the unfairness of being banished from your own land.

'I didn't go out often, because it was a five-ten-minute walk to Rosa's. I'd think, "Do I really want to go?" Then I had to say hello to her, obviously, out of politeness, and then again, when I got back, and I had to walk back from there, so it was very inconvenient. Sometimes I thought, "Can I be bothered?" And so then, I was even more trapped in my home,' Sarah says, matter-of-factly.

Out of gratitude, and perhaps pity for poor Rosa, who led a life of downtrodden servitude in an all-male household, Sarah offered to help with the grape harvest.

*

The *vendemmia* (grape harvest), so beloved of filmmakers for the opportunities to photograph blissful golden romance among the black and green brilliance of the vines, was backbreaking and filthy. Sarah came home exhausted every day.

Day after day, from eight o'clock in the morning until seven o'clock at night, with an hour and a half for lunch, Sarah bent to snip the bunches of grapes with her secateurs. Bending and snipping, snipping and bending, bending and snipping. And when she dropped a grape, she had to bend twice or three times, to retrieve that grape, put it into the basket. And pluck the mouldy bunches too. Carrying and weighing, weighing and carrying. All under that hot, unforgiving sun.

It wasn't only the sun that was unforgiving. Sarah soon realised that as an inexperienced grape picker (and a woman), she was bottom of the pecking order.

One of the older workers, a *contadino* who had farmed in the area from boyhood and was significantly older than Sarah, insisted that the man follow the woman. And why would this be, Sarah wondered, although she already knew. That old genetic inferiority again. Evidently, women would be incapable of ensuring that all the grapes were picked. They would miss bunches. And they wouldn't be doing it in the correct fashion. After all, there was a distinct way of cutting bunches that a woman would not, could not, just simply *did* not know.

The younger *contadini* were different. They were impressed by Sarah's speed and unconvinced of her inexperience. They thought she had been picking grapes for years. One grape picker from abroad was simply disdainful of everyone, whatever their gender or length of time served. He insisted on inspecting every bunch and removing unripe or overripe grapes.

The days were long.

Lunchtime. Ah lunchtime.

Rosa cooked every day, serving her food to the starving grape pickers who sat round the oil cloth-covered table in the dim kitchen, their bodies steaming as they cooled off. Sarah's tiredness shielded her from feelings of discomfort, being surrounded by people she didn't know well. And every day, the food Rosa served up was: a big bowl of pasta, accompanied by a *brasato*—a piece of braised beef— or sometimes a breaded, flattened pork chop, and in the middle of the table, bottles of rough, homemade red wine. The menu never varied. Every day, pasta and *brasato*…

About two weeks into the picking, and two weeks into the never varying lunches, Rosa's husband Giovanni came into the kitchen, leaned into the centre of the table, hopeful in spite of himself, and lifted the lid off the crusty old ceramic pot containing the slabs of meat.

'*Cristo*,' (Christ,) he exploded.

The wine was a consolation. It washed everything down comfortably. Too comfortably for Giovanni. The old man liked to keep a tight hold of outgoings, including the wine disappearing down the throats of his workforce. He was not rich. The farm had to support him and Rosa and their son. It was a hard living, the one they scratched from this beautiful land.

One of the workers in Sarah's gang liked to get drunk.

'*Non permetto certe cose. Venga a lavorare*,' (I'm not having this. He came to work,) said Giovanni, his gravelly voice rising.

Sarah was in the kitchen ahead of the others, chatting companionably with Rosa before lunch. Rosa didn't let her help. Everything was laid out on the newspaper covering the table on which she prepared that day's *brasato* and pasta. They had no hot running water. All the cooking was done on a wood-burning stove, lit throughout winter and summer, into which Rosa continuously fed logs, branches, scraps of old cartons and wooden pallets to maintain the temperature. She didn't use gloves. The skin on her red and flaking hands was sufficiently hardened that she barely noticed the splintery scrapings of the wood as she shoved them into the old stove.

Sarah watched as Giovanni thrust out his spade-shaped hands to grab a couple of the half-full wine bottles on the table. He jammed a plastic funnel into each bottle in turn and poured in water, shook the bottles slightly, then replaced them in the middle of the table.

When the others filed in to take their seats, the drunk— a middle-aged man with a rounded *pancia* (belly) that looked incongruous bulging out from his spindly frame—reached for the bottle. He was not fooled by the stream of light red liquid flowing into his glass. He held the bottle up to the domed lamp that cast a dim light over the table, examined it intently, shook it and declared, indignantly, *'C'è acqua in questo vino.'* (There's water in this wine.)

*

'It was awful, awful work,' says Sarah now.

Giovanni's careful managing of the family's income meant he quickly accepted Sarah's offer of working for half the pay of the other pickers. After all, they were letting her park her car there for free. Sarah presented this argument to him, only half expecting him to agree. When he did, she found herself working for 2.5 euros an hour, for ten hours a day.

Giovanni and Rosa had land, a solid house, but their living was hard and the memories lingered of the poverty shared by many of their generation. Rosa threw nothing away. Her husband's jacket was a coat of many patches, which Sarah admired. She complimented Giovanni on his designer clothes. Everything was made with local materials. Everything was made to last. Things could be adjusted, mended, re-used. It was so in tune with Sarah's philosophy of living, which was evolving as the months and years passed in this, her beloved country.

Harvesting the grapes, however, finally proved too much. She decided to stop the grape picking after about three seasons, much to Giovanni's consternation. He begged her to do the grape harvest again, but Sarah was adamant.

'My body just could not take it anymore,' she says now, but when she said this to Giovanni, he could not understand.

'*Ah, ma tu sei piu giovane di me,*' (Ah, but you are younger than me,) he protested, spreading his great hands into a cradling cup as if trying to hold on to something.

'It's your life. It's not my life,' she retorted, in her direct fashion, necessary in part because of her limited Italian, but also a reflection of her growing self-assurance and sense of belonging. At this point, she was feeling that the language was hers to manipulate, rather than the other way round. Italian no longer daunted her, even if the local dialect often remained impenetrable.

Giovanni had to accept regretfully—she was very quick and, indeed, very cheap.

By this time, in any case, the plan Sarah had been incubating as a solution to the scourge of the reign of *Cattivo* was ready for birth. If *Cattivo* wouldn't leave her alone, she would turn her back on him.

CHAPTER 13 *bis*

Luke makes this alternative to Rosa's braised beef, which might be more appetising:

Brasato di manzo (braised beef or pot roast).

This is a traditional dish from the area, 'very soft and delicate,' says Luke. It has been called la ricetta piemontese per eccellenza (the pre-eminent Piedmont recipe).

Luke uses a good but slightly tough piece of meat with a lot of fat and sinew, avoiding leaner cuts. The meat is slow cooked, allowing time for the fat and sinew to break down and keep the meat juicy. The meat can be marinaded beforehand with the usual suspects: chopped onions, carrots and celery, along with whole garlic cloves, some whole peppercorns and maybe bay leaves. Because it is lighter, Luke uses Arneis white wine, rather than one of the more typical reds: Barbaresco, Barolo or Barbera.

The meat is strained before putting it in the cooking pot and the wine sauce is poured over the meat. Luke seasons the dish, cooking the meat slowly on top of the stove for about four hours.

*

It used to be a tradition in the neighbourhood that older people, those over sixty-five, were given a box of food at Christmas, 'in the good old days before austerity.' Luke is not sure how widespread this custom was, but in any case, this community largesse has disappeared.

Rosa and Giovanni used to receive pasta, but it was not their usual pasta, nor the right thickness. Rosa didn't want to waste the pasta, but served it to her men, husband and son, with trepidation.

The two men started shouting at Rosa. '*Non la mangerò questa pasta. Voglio la mia pasta normale.*' (I'm not eating this pasta. I want my normal pasta.)

'Sometimes you can hear them shouting from here,' says Luke.

'Husband or son?' I ask.

'Son.'

'He shouts at his mother?'

'But she loves him to death. Mollycoddles him.'

'How old is he?'

'Fifty-four.'

CHAPTER 14
Building the Wall—a new beginning

The film Fitzcarraldo, made by German director Werner Herzog in 1982, tells the story of an eccentric Irishman Brian Sweeney Fitzgerald, who sought his fortune as a rubber baron in the Peruvian Amazon. The film, loosely based on a true story, documents moving a 340-tonne steam ship over a mountain without the use of special effects. While there never was a Brian Sweeney Fitzgerald in Peru and no one (except for Herzog) ever tried to move an intact 340-tonne steam ship over a mountain, there was a Peruvian named Carlos Fermin Fitzcarrald, a rubber baron who lived in Iquitos. He was the son of an American (not Irish) father and a Peruvian mother. Indeed, Fitzcarrald did move a steam ship over a mountain, but not before it had been dismantled so that it could be taken over piece by piece.

Herzog by contrast directed an indigenous crew to transport the entire ship intact over the mountain. Extreme ambition…

What do you do with a problem like Cattivo? If you're Sarah, you dream the impossible dream. She is Fitzcarraldo.

Piedmont
Spring 2008

This feeling of being trapped could not continue. Sarah's world shrank. It had to stop. It had to.

Their friend Richard, who had driven the van containing Sarah and Luke's old life to their new life here, would arrive that evening with his wife Grace. Luke had just had a birthday and it had become a tradition to celebrate it at *Cascina Cannella* with their oldest friends. They were proud of how they had upheld this tradition, despite the physical distance between them.

Sarah loved Richard and Grace. She and Luke had been planning the menus and trips for weeks, and anticipated with pleasure the reminiscences they would share. She gardened furiously. Everything reached towards the sun and warmth. They had all—plants, humans and cats—weathered a particularly fierce snow-filled winter, the snow drifts piling up to over one metre. The earth was soft now and pregnable. All life beneath was bursting to escape. It was Sarah's vocation to manage the vegetation, to sculpt and trim until the garden resembled the image she carried with her in her mind's eye.

Buried layers deep—so many layers—that wretched piece of grit irritated the completeness of her contentment. Where would they park their car? If they parked in the driveway, for sure *Cattivo* would come out to complain. He would bring out his two Belgian shepherds with their teeth yellow against the darkness of their pointed muzzles, their thick tongues lolling. This was not the welcome she wanted for their guests.

Richard and Grace would stay in the upstairs apartment, built in place of the old hayloft, the one they claimed as theirs as soon as it was built. It had become their home from home. The double folding shutters were of heavy louvered beechwood, stained a dark forest green and furnished with wrought iron rods and rings to close them. They folded against the end wall of the apartment and were secured with black iron knobs that looked like the upper half of a man, with shoulders and head. The head had to be pulled up to allow the body to slot neatly into place. Outside was the balcony, with three sides open to the surrounding hills and the never-ending breadth of the sky.

Sarah loved these details. What colour should the shutters be stained? How would they fit effectively into the space? How should they be fastened? She started with the detail and worked her way towards the big picture. If the detail was incorrect, she strove to make it conform to her vision. And as the house recovered from the years of dereliction, Sarah took the greatest pleasure in the small, but perfect, finishing touches—a line of pink ochre painted as straight as the flight of an arrow along the bottom of a wall, in imitation of a detail seen in a local church; the satin feel of the original wooden hand-rail up the staircase, its splintery grey surface now sanded, polished and soft under the skin of your fingers.

Sarah enjoyed preparing the rooms, opening wide the windows and balcony doors to reveal the views onto the courtyard and the valley beneath. She loved lifting the fresh bed linen, so that it flew up to gulp in the air before coming to rest on the bed. She loved smoothing out the creases, puffing up the pillows. She loved the feeling of anticipation, the lead-up to these visits.

When she had finished, with everything in place, she stepped through the double doors just beyond the foot of the bed onto the small balcony (so many balconies), and surveyed her garden, her land, her *terra*. The breeze was up as usual, frothing the foliage. She leaned on the railing, lifted her face to the sun. Still moments like this were becoming rare. She was finding herself in demand among people with holiday homes here as someone who could coordinate and oversee building work, and, importantly, translate not just the language but the underlying spirit of the language, what the words *really* meant. She was even making money. Slowly, but steadily, this reserved but resolute woman was making a name for herself.

Only one thing was causing the surface of her contentment to ripple...

*

Of all the things you might wonder about or fear when considering a change of country, a feuding neighbour would probably not be top of the list. Sarah and Luke had never imagined a scenario where their lives would be under the control of someone they had never met, whose path they had never crossed and who seemed as susceptible to reason as a mud pie. Why, why? Why wasn't *il Cattivo* like the Rossis, offering gifts and bonhomie and advice—and vegetables, so many vegetables? *Signor* Rossi was never satisfied with the quantity of produce grown on Sarah and Luke's *orto*, and continued to provide them with huge quantities of vegetables from his *orto*. Sarah and Luke, meanwhile, were able throughout the winter to live off the vast batches of tomato sauce they made from their own tomatoes. *Signor* Rossi didn't eat a lot himself, his teeth were quite sparse. He had a good round *pancia* (belly) for such a sprightly man and claimed it was because of all the bread he ate, '*non mangerò se non c'è del pane.*' (I won't eat if there's no bread).

The relationship with *Signor* Rossi continued to be a very fruitful one for them all.

It wasn't only in the area of food that *Signor* Rossi proved such a good and useful neighbour. He had also noticed that Luke and Sarah's plot had lots of old wood lying around and they had arrived one holiday, before the permanent move to Italy, to find that the fires had been laid ready to go. And *Signor* Rossi continued to keep them warm through the winters even after they had made the big move. He delivered tractor loads of wood from his land as payment for the grapes from the vines. Apart from vegetables and wood, he also delivered the many heavy stones on his land, which could be put to effective use in creating the garden. Luke and Sarah would gather these into piles and *Signor* Rossi would bring them round once again on his tractor.

Tiny Sofia, *Signor* Rossi's wife, hurled these weighty stones around as if they were mere pebbles, despite suffering a disorder that she said made her feel tired. Sarah was impressed, 'the average person would not manage half the physical work she did in a day.' Sofia might have been a model for Sarah whose physical labouring on *Cascina Cannella* was legendary in the locality.

Il Cattivo was no Rossi. Sarah and Luke had, somehow, to decrease his inordinate interference in their lives. They didn't want to be obliged to modify their behaviour at every turn to mollify him. His dominance disturbed their self-assurance. They felt invaded. And Sarah especially did not want him crouching, unbidden, in her head. He had to be banished.

Sarah thought about his tomatoes. Vast numbers of tomatoes dripping from the vines, planted right next to the wall they had built to support their raised vegetable plot on the hillside. The wall bordered on the neighbour's land, to which he had no objection, but he harried them and their builders to resettle the earth. '*Veloci, veloci ragazzi. Voglio piantare i miei pomodori,*' (hurry up, hurry up lads. I want to plant my tomatoes,) he urged, clapping his hands. The builders laughed and gave him short shrift, '*bene, vai al supermercato,*' (well, go to the supermarket). The tomatoes were planted and grew and fruited copiously at the foot of the wall, but they were never harvested. Sarah watched them rot, sadly. *Il Cattivo* was driven to plant the tomatoes (and drove everyone else). It was the season for planting tomatoes. But to no end. No one ate the tomatoes. This grieved Sarah.

They tried changing the doors, switching the main entrance to the house from beside the driveway to the kitchen side, where you can step, unwatched, directly into the protection of the courtyard. They tried blocking views, with exuberantly growing plants. They tried making access difficult, installing a two-metre high black steel double gate at the mouth of the driveway, then covering it with fast-growing golden heart ivy. These measures were not enough.

The idea of a possible solution grew slowly, but insistently, as the months and years went by and the house and land became increasingly theirs to protect and nurture.

What they did, finally, was more magnificent than anything else that went before.

They created a place that *turned its back on the neighbour*. They took the location and put it back to front. And the driving force behind this decision was Sarah.

*

Project Wall was born. If *il Cattivo* would not leave them alone, then they would banish him from view. The house stood a short distance from the mountain road. They would build their private driveway, by carving out a vast wall that would curve around the house in a protective and impregnable embrace. This was the maddest project of them all, but it had to be done.

Even Luke thought the idea was too ambitious—and expensive—but Sarah was dogged. She could not be persuaded to give it up.

One evening in late May during one of my recent 'working' visits (such hard work), the air still quite warm, we are sitting on the end balcony, eating one of Luke's delicious dinners. It is dark, and the ever-present breeze ruffles our hair and the fabric of our light cotton tops—we are after all on a high hilltop and the breeze is our constant, indeed welcome, companion. We are gazing out at the random lights dotted over the hillsides surrounding us, contented, sipping on a light Dolcetto. I don't want to spoil this contentment, but I am curious. I dare to ask Sarah the obvious, but difficult, question, that is—whether, at any point, she had thought about leaving—even if not the country, then at least *Cascina Cannella*—maybe starting afresh in another house, on another piece of land, in another neighbourhood.

To my surprise, she says yes.

'Two or three times, I've sat up there and thought, "I can't do this anymore." Because there used to be times I'd go out—Luke wasn't here—and I'd see him (*il Cattivo*) around that entrance, the old entrance, the only one at that time, and I'd think, I can't go back. I can't go past that man. I used to dread coming home; thinking, is he going to be there? Is he going to be there waiting around? You would see this face at the window… ' She trails off. The tendons in her neck remain taut.

'Can you pinpoint when you made that decision to build the road? Because that's a huge project.' We are back on track, no longer sucked into the depressing *Cattivo* mire, but discussing how to solve the problem, much more to Sarah and Luke's taste.

'After we'd finished the building work on the house, we decided to build the road, because we'd had enough. I mean, it wasn't just leaving my car at Giovanni and Rosa's house for three years. There was never room for me. And he would always complain. Every time friends came, it was a struggle for them to park. We needed to do something. Every time we had a visitor, it was such a pain to think: "Oh God, where are they going to park their car? I hope they don't park it on the road, because he'll just come out and complain." You would see their faces…' Sarah stops, remembering. 'So that had to stop. That had to stop…'

Worst of all, Sarah and Luke were taking out their frustrations on each other. 'The arguments always, always came down to the neighbour, every time, always him.' What to do about him, how to circumvent him, how to live with the fact of him. Their relationship, the bedrock of this life, was foundering.

'It's not what you want.' They smile at each other, somewhat ruefully. Then Daisy drawls, raising her glass (containing a fine dry Roero Arneis white wine): 'Well, he (*Cattivo*) ain't worth it.' We all laugh. He certainly ain't.

*

Project Wall was turning into an administrative black hole.

The *geometra* Luke and Sarah had hired to sort out the documents, *Signor* Merlo, was getting cold feet. He and Sarah were sitting in the cool of the kitchen at the rectangular wooden table, which Sarah had created from an old door and that now gleamed softly in the shafts of sunlight entering the narrow windows on either side of the counter. They were gazing at the different piles of paperwork. *Signor* Merlo was a middle-aged, nervous man with a light smattering of ill-defined moustache. His rather small hands were hovering over each pile in turn, as if they themselves were made nervous about the weight and volume of the information beneath them.

Sarah was fixing him with her gimlet eye. He seemed to be shrinking before her.

'*È un lavoro importante, un grande lavoro,*' (it's a big job, a big job,) he said mournfully, hands fluttering. '*Vi costera un sacco di soldi,*' (it's going to cost you a lot of money).

Sarah replied as forcefully as she could. 'But we've got to do it. Please tell me how much it costs and what we need to get.' She was imploring now.

The *geometra's* hands stopped fluttering. He pushed himself up from the table. '*Non ho molta esperienza in questo genere de cose. Troverò qualcun altro,*' (I'm not experienced in this kind of thing; I'll find you somebody else.)

Two years. For two years *Signor* Merlo had supposedly been organising the paperwork.

*

'I'm not kidding. Two years—and I was going mad, mad, *mad*, all with not very good Italian.' Sarah is even now raking her slender fingers through her hair as she recollects —luckily, we haven't eaten the mussels yet; fishy hair is not good.

I broach the subject of money, tentatively.

'It was such a massive project. I know you'd sold up in England—but there must have been money worries?'

Daisy pipes up, 'Didn't that cost as much as everything else?' She is adept at steering a path through the serious and the comic.

'Yes it did—because the whole wall had to be done.' Sarah struggles to find a way of conveying the enormity of the project. 'It wasn't just a case of... It was this big, big movement of land.' She spreads her arms wide, 'huge movement of land. Ah no, it was huge.' She is picturing it, the mountains of stones, the tonnages of earth and rubble, the sheer, mad ambition.

'The locals wondered what the hell were we doing—because it wasn't obvious at the beginning... not at all.'

Eventually, they settled on a young and zealously efficient *geometra,* a young woman fresh out of university, who wanted to make certain that the wall wouldn't fall down.

'It's got so much metal, it could probably go on to Calais. It was ridiculous, just ridiculous. Cost us a fortune, more than it should have,' says Sarah. The infectiousness of her laughter invites us to join. So it cost them a fortune, so what, *tanto peggio.* The relief, the release, the marvellous freedom.

Because of the project management work she does for others in the area, Sarah now has a great network of Italian builders, plumbers, electricians, gardeners and yes, *geometras.* This morning she received a phone call from one of her 'clients,' a Norwegian man who has just bought a holiday house a few valleys away. Will she take care of the imminent delivery of a fridge? He's calling from Vietnam...

Both the foreigners who seek escape in Italy and the locals who know they will be treated respectfully and, importantly, will be paid, trust her. She seems more at home, more relaxed with her local acquaintances and contacts in the building trade than with many others. She has learnt the proverbial tricks. She too climbs the scaffolding and does the physical work.

She speaks the language.

When they embarked on Project Wall, all hands were turned to moving the earth, to excavating this land, to decapitating the top of their hillside. It was like a grand municipal construction project. Two building teams were involved who did not always agree. This rivalry worked to everyone's advantage. The project expanded, drawing in the community. Local people, even people they barely knew, came with their tractors to help clear the debris and the dug-up earth and to pick up the excavated stones. Where should the stones be stored? They would be needed later. Places had to be found to keep them. They were piled in the vineyard, against walls, in layer upon layer against the stone staircase leading to the newly built apartment.

'We were a bit naïve,' says Sarah, 'we should have organised big lorries to clear the mounds of excavations.' But she is not sorry about that failure to foresee the immense amounts of necessary materials. The project became a joint venture with their neighbours, forging another ironclad link to this land. Before Sarah and Luke set off upon this imaginative act of self-renewal, they had not realised how much it would embed them in the community. The sour relationship with one close neighbour was being drained of its bitterness through the sweet sensation of real belonging and friendship.

This did not mean that everyone was wholeheartedly approving, nor entirely convinced of their English neighbours' sanity...

The wall cost 18,000 euros, but this sum did not include either the moving of land, or the opposing wall on the other side of the road. Nor the stonework facing necessary to mitigate the wall's forbidding profile and lend it the character and beauty appropriate to the surrounding landscape. The job was going to cost them another 11,000 euros. Sarah did the maths.

Luke invited his eighteen-year old nephew, Oskar, to spend the summer working on their building site. Oskar is Michael's son, who was living at that time with his Danish mother in Denmark. Oskar takes after his mother. He is fair, with blue-grey eyes and the charisma of a thoughtful man. At eighteen, he was excited to be spending a summer in Italy, with his extended family, earning money. It was the perfect arrangement..

*

After the years Sarah had spent avoiding *il Cattivo*, today held the promise of an end to his tyranny. She bent to attack the pile of stones on the ground with delight, picking the ones to fit the space that remained on the last unfaced part of the interminable wall that would be her assurance of freedom. Sarah had chosen each stone to place on the cement surface of the wall, to give it the proper, finished look. It had to be in tune with the house, which she and Peter had stripped of peeling plaster and repointed, stone by stone, over four long months several *Piemontese* summers ago.

Menta joined her, making happy cat noises as she wove between Sarah's legs, tickling her ankles with her colourful fur. She was every type of tabby, spotted, striped and white with one eye lined in black and the other in pink. She had been found on a tomb in the local cemetery, a noisy little bundle of fluffy kitten. Ever since they had brought her home—some years ago now—wherever Sarah went, she would follow. In tune with their tradition, they named her after another herb, Mint.

'*Ciao Menta,* how are you today?' Sarah leaned to give the cat's ears a gentle tug. *Menta* continued to make delicate figures of eight around her ankles, as Sarah went back to digging into the pile of stones. She was remembering how she and Luke had embarked on this project—this *crazy* project, in the eyes of their neighbours who shared with them the mountaintop in northern Italy and who weren't shy about offering advice or pithy observations. 'Oh you haven't got enough stones' was a favourite.

Did she have enough stones? This worried Sarah, although she never responded. And at the end, once all the facing was done, once they had downed tools, disposed of the leftover cement, and assimilated the enormity of the completed task, all they had left were two car loads.

Oskar came over to talk to the cat and to take a break from the backbreaking work under the burning summer sun. He was skinny and as brown as a nut, a taller version of Sarah. She had taught him how to make the cement, but had not allowed him to choose the stones nor to place them on the wall. These were her tasks, hers alone.

He crouched to tickle *Menta* under the chin, grateful to be able to stretch his body.

'Are you going to watch us cement the last stone, little cat?'

Here they were, at the far end of the freshly faced wall. *Menta* lost interest, wandering off, as Sarah turned her attention to choosing the last stone for its shape, colour and size. Using the small ruler, she calculated the space left.

There, it was done.

Sarah stood straight, lengthening her bruised body and stretching her arms to the sky, uncurling her fingers. Arthritis. No wonder her body was shot. She'd shifted twenty-two tonnes of stone in four months to build a wall fifty metres long and 1.6 metres high. Bits of stone and cement still clung to her shortish blond hair.

It was time to take stock.

No more disputes, no more spying, no more creeping about calculating how to avoid him, no more sudden shocks as he materialised at her shoulder. Sarah would cut herself off from him, keep him out. No more *il Cattivo*.

She and Oskar sat on the bank, earth hard beneath their bottoms and their backs against the wall, breathing in the air. Through half closed eyes, Sarah noticed *Menta* coming back towards them from the opposite side of the road, where the mountain dropped steeply. She had chosen to cross the road at the point where it curved around the hazelnut grove. As *Menta* started to trot happily towards Sarah, a car came at speed around the bend from the direction of the old driveway and in a single moment—the space of an intake of breath—killed the cat with the fifty-seven varieties of fluffy tabby fur, her constant companion.

Sarah's triumph was extinguished with him.

CHAPTER 14 *bis*
Due antipasti (two starters)

Slices of courgette, lightly sautéed in olive oil and sprinkled with fresh Parmesan cheese

Cozze gratinate (mussels au gratin)

Luke puts the mussels into a large pot with white wine and steams them for a few minutes on a fairly high heat until they have all opened. He then sets them aside to cool and saves the liquor. The topping for the mussels is made by mixing breadcrumbs, pepperoncino, garlic and parsley, all blended together with a little bit of oil. Luke then adds the mussel liquor, which has been concentrated down by at least half. Once the mussels have cooled down, he removes the top of the shell and covers the mussels with the topping. He then grills them or puts them in the oven. Eh voilà!

The correct type of pasta to be used with particular sauces is the subject of much study, debate, controversy and excitement. This is not something a non-Italian ever succeeds in understanding. Even Luke, practically a native, has given up the notion of having full mastery of the pasta knowledge.

After a wine-tasting event with friends one evening, Luke and one of the friends, an American named Amy, offered to make everyone an impromptu supper. Among their group, which included a diverse range of nationalities, was a smart Italian man, the smooth Leonardo, a guest of one of the group. As they whipped up a bowl of pasta with broccoli, Luke had a suspicion of what might come next.

When you have broccoli in the sauce, you should always serve it with *orecchiette* pasta from Puglia (literally, little ears). But of course, this was an impromptu supper and they didn't have any *orecchiette*. As they served up the pasta dish, Luke whispered to Amy: 'Leonardo's not going to be happy, he's going to have the Italian pasta police onto us because we're serving it with *penne* (standard pasta tubes).'

And sure enough, as they put the food onto the table, Leonardo protested vigorously, '*E il tipo sbagliato di pasta.*' (This is the wrong type of pasta.) '*Dovremmo avere le orecchiette.*' (We should have *orecchiette.*)

CHAPTER 15
The Crafted Piece: Becoming Sarah

Building a wall does not usually signify greater freedom for anyone, quite the opposite. The Berlin wall was not designed to bring freedom. US President Trump did not propose a wall along the border between the USA and Mexico to make people happy. Israel's wall fed fear and hatred.

Paradoxically, in the case of Sarah and Luke, the building of the great wall brought freedom and happiness. The wall and the shiny new driveway that curves steeply upwards towards *Cascina Cannella* like the stairway to heaven meant a fresh beginning for them, but especially for Sarah. *Il Cattivo* could torment her no more. She could stand at the crest of the driveway, one hand on her hip, the other shading her eyes, and survey the surrounding hills with a sense of peace and order. Most comforting of all, she would be able to come and go as she pleased, park where she wished. They had, quite simply, put him behind them.

The place was still a building site, however.

Along either side of the driveway lay soil that had been used as a dump for the debris, for stones and any old rubbish generated during the great project. Would anything ever grow there?

As Sarah walked along her wall, surveying the workmanship, admiring its curve, she kicked randomly at one or two bits of rubble. When she bent to look more closely at the stones, she discovered different threads of colour that made paler streaks through the hard dark-grey surface. Picking them up, she turned them over, examined their unique patterns, thinking not of their function nor of where to put them, but simply of their shapes and colours.

The wall also brought freedom of a different kind—artistic freedom. With the transformation of the house into a home of beauty and the land into a more manageable state, Sarah's imagination was wandering. The renovations had unearthed her creativity. Building the wall had revealed both creativity and a useful stubborn streak. She would need new outlets for them both. She was open to any new opportunities…

Balconies and business

For most, one balcony would be a luxury. Sarah and Luke have three.

These balconies exactly illustrate the key to this place of beauty—planning, an ability to imagine, even in the midst of degradation and ruined buildings and scrubland, what could be created. Sarah, in particular, has the ability to start with the important detail and mentally picture how that can be made to fit into the whole. Artistry and practicality go hand in hand: making sure a shutter opens in the right way, creating a soft planting area in a hard stone and concrete surround, envisaging how light will fall in a room. The big picture only grows from these details.

'I think I can definitely see things at the end from the beginning. I know what I want to achieve and I can see the finished result, so I can plan in very fine detail from the beginning where I want things.'

Sarah's father liked to paint in his spare time, and she wonders (occasionally, and not regretfully) whether she should have chosen an artistic path rather than a more scientific one when she was young. It was more logical to bend towards the science side when she was choosing her future. She saw this as a more effective means to get a job, earn a good living—and 'there was no such job as a designer then.' Now, she believes her creative side has always been the stronger part of her character.

Through friends—drawn from a wide pool of local Italians as well as settlers from further afield—Sarah's name and reputation spread. She found herself increasingly in demand from people who had bought holiday homes in Italy. First of all, they wanted advice. This soon escalated into asking Sarah to liaise between them and her Italian contacts. As her command of Italian improved, she became more relaxed and contented in the company of people she called on both for advice and help in getting jobs done. Her responsibilities grew until she was taking control of aspects of maintenance or refurbishment. And then, ultimately, she was entrusted with the wholesale design of the renovations, along with management of the work, and installation of the new fittings—glass doors for the bathroom, machined to the most precise thickness; tiles for the kitchen floor; concealed lighting.

One friend and customer asked her to design their entire garden.

On a visit, Sarah asks me if I want to accompany her to see one or two of the houses she oversees. Of course I do. We rattle up and down the winding roads towards the first one. I am staring fixedly ahead as these bends and curves and the occasional rapid braking in the face of a wide vehicle coming the other way make me nauseous. Sarah is oblivious and wields her car confidently along these highways. We approach the house from the lower part of the hill, so that it looms ever larger. It is a vast building carving out a sharply delineated rectangle against the blue skyscape. Outside is evidence of excavations—mounds of rubble dumped on the scrubby patch of land where nothing now grows. The rocks and earth have been dug out from the side of the hill to create a giant hole, mimicking the rectangular shape of the house itself. The householders, a husband and wife who live in Germany with their three young children, are having a swimming pool built. The wife visits often with the children, expecting everything to be in order on arrival and leaving everything in disorder on departure. They are people for whom being serviced is the natural way of life—not super-rich, but modern and affluent Europeans who simply do not consider clearing up after themselves, even leaving the fridge full of food (which Sarah does not waste).

We enter the house via a set of solid concrete steps. Inside, it is particularly cool after the intensity of the heat outside. The high-ceilinged rooms are also long rectangles, lined in a single row, so that you could ride your bicycle from one end to the other. It made me think of *The Shining* and the small boy who rides his tricycle around the long corridors of a deserted hotel, snowed in for the winter and cut off from the rest of the world.

Furniture is sparse. Personal artefacts are few. The only feature that gives this building any interest is the cellar, with its unplastered stone walls and vaulted brick ceiling. Outside again, we bask in the sunshine after the chill of the cold, unwelcoming house. The land that isn't covered by swimming pool excavations runs downwards towards the road, bare of planting except for tangles of desiccated brown stems and withered leaves, turned crisp by the heat. Sarah's principal task, apart from general management of the servicing, is to oversee the construction of the pool. She is content to do this, but the work does not feed her soul.

We make one more sortie, this time to her favourite house, owned by a British couple with whom she has become good friends. This has an entirely different atmosphere. The house is just as solid as the previous one, but does not dominate the skyline, instead nestling unobtrusively against the slope. Inside, the rooms do not reveal themselves immediately—no manic bicycle-riding here, there are too many hidden staircases, too many corners to negotiate. You walk down a small flight of rough stone steps to the kitchen, which feels cool and welcoming and functional, with its tiled floor, dimpled and faded in places where feet have worn away the terracotta.

It is for this house Sarah will create a new garden from the largely bare earth. They want flowers, lots of flowers; she suggests a more mixed style of planting, including herbs, to suit the landscape and conditions. They entrust her with their dreams, as well as their money.

The crafted piece has the ability to be unique

This practical work for others, interesting, demanding and stimulating (and sometimes daunting) though it was, did not fulfil that tentative yearning Sarah felt towards something less tangible, more purely artistic and completely her own.

It always starts with the materials—the rusting metal head of an old hoe, the ruined grey wood of a discarded door.

When she first set foot in her Italian future, Sarah was entranced by the beauty of the materials—stones lying in the fields or bits of metal beside the road, 'I always thought they were beautiful.' Behind the object lies a story. For Sarah, part of the attraction of taking the discarded artefacts and the decaying materials and refashioning them into something new is the sense of continuity with the past. Museums can be sad places because they 'recreate the past, they don't move it on.'

When Sarah takes that pointed metal head of a disused shovel and makes it part of a crafted piece of ingenuity and charm—the long spine of a fish, for example, topped with a shovel snout—she is offering us the chance to laugh and find joy. The worn-out shovel is no longer a reminder of decay, of time passing and things (people) no longer useful, but a source of pleasure.

'If you take an object that somebody made—and obviously spent a lot of time making it—and turn it into something else that someone can use now, it then becomes something pleasurable. It hasn't been burnt on the fire or thrown on a rubbish tip. It hasn't died. And the person who made it hasn't died. The person who sat there for hours and hours, whittling away or whatever, that person is still living.'

A friend in the wine trade ('a handsome brute,' says Luke) produces wine from vineyards planted in four different places in the region. He was looking for a way to display four different types of soil to customers. Sarah took a large stave from a very old wine barrel and attached springs. Each bottle, containing the soil, is held in each of the springs. The handsome brute, who became a father for the first time after the age of fifty ('he looks a bit knackered now') bought this 'display case' for his shop, making his payment in wine rather than cash.

Such serendipitous meetings occur frequently, but Sarah is also growing more bold in seeking out places to exhibit her work.

One day, she went to a local community meeting where people were discussing the approaching annual town festival. She took a couple of simple pieces she had made —a candle holder wrought from a piece of metal beaten into shape, the rusty surface made smooth, and a picture frame made from two L-shaped black metal hinges, hooked together to form a rectangle. She showed them to the town mayor, an ebullient man whose excitement was intoxicating. He happily passed the objects around the room, urging people to admire them. Sarah realised she wasn't just 'making rubbish' but producing things people liked.

A room at the museum was given to her to fill as she wished. She called it her *esposizione di riciclaggio* (recycling exhibition). She whitewashed the walls in light colours; cleaned the tile floor of its accumulated dirt; created her own display tables from ramshackle bits of wood, now finely sanded and oiled, and hung pieces on the walls.

The work can be demanding physically. Sarah's hands are more worn than the rest of her body, their lines and pathways and calloused skin a testimony to her craftsmanship. She works with a blacksmith to bend the metal components to her design. All the scraping and cleaning, the meticulous sanding and surface preparation, she does herself. This is work that satisfies her soul.

Sarah looks at an object, turns it over in her hands, feels its texture, imagines another function for it. A prosaic object becomes important because it is an individual creation. She remains full of admiration for the original crafted piece.

'People who made those things were incredibly skilful. They made things to last, to be mended. I'm just mending them in a different way. I use the skill of the person who made it in the first place. I am making a "jigsaw".'

*

The future

Sarah's exhibition at the local museum was just the start of a more public life for her creations. They began to attract attention. Gradually, they started to leave home. From *Cascina Cannella*, they moved into the houses of her friends in Italy; then further afield into the houses of her friends and family in England. As their circle of admirers widened, the crafted objects set foot tentatively into the big wide world.

When Sarah received the email from someone whose name was at first unfamiliar, she was puzzled. What was this? A new exhibition? In a town she didn't know well, far from home? And then, as she remembered, her disbelief grew. The email was from one of the artists she had met about a year and a half ago at a previous exhibition—her first such show after the *esposizione di riciclaggio*. It was held in the crypt of an old church in a neighbouring large town.

A simple get-together of local artists, informal, no big deal. Afterwards, they had kept in sporadic touch. And now, here in her mailbox, was an invitation to show her work in a much larger, much more public space—in an old *palazzo* (palace) that dates back to Roman times.

Sarah accepted immediately, nervous but exhilarated.

The *palazzo* stole her breath. She and Luke had made the journey there to check out the space. Four storeys high with three internal courtyards and a neglected garden, a tangle of dull grey-green leaves and stalks and stems in browns and yellows, the *palazzo* set Sarah's imagination on fire. As she descended into the great arched cellars, where the group of artists will show their work, she could already see where a piece might fit, where another might startle.

New exhibitions are scheduled in larger towns. There are new commissions, as Sarah approaches this restaurant or that shop owner, most often with success. She has also been commissioned to design the shop window of a bespoke kitchen maker, using her pieces to furnish the show kitchen. And a man much impressed by a small wall cupboard designed and built by Sarah made an hour-long trip to collect it, with a request for further pieces.

Not only has *Cascina Cannella* been transformed. So has Sarah.

CHAPTER 15 *bis*

From the private... this *finestra chiusa* (closed window) now hangs on my wall. It is one of the first pieces Sarah displayed publicly when she initially exhibited her work in the local museum, her *esposizione di riciclaggio* (recycling exhibition).

...To the public—this shovel head fish hangs in a local restaurant. Sarah plucked up her courage and talked to the restaurant owner about displaying one of her pieces. The owner was more than happy to hang it in a prominent position. Local people and tourists constantly pass by the piece. Sarah is thrilled and slightly incredulous—can this really be her, living this life?

CHAPTER 16
Enter Allegra

Piedmont
Summer 2013

Sarah would not be talked into it.

Luke could think of nothing else.

'Sarah, just promise me you'll think about it, at least that.'

Sarah turned from him, arms crossed tight around her body.

'I have to check the vines.'

Sarah and Luke had been together ever since they met at university, both eighteen and fresh in the world. And here they were, living the life Luke had always dreamed of, high on a mountaintop in rural Italy. He had already asked much of Sarah. Thirty years on, he knew exactly what he was asking of her now.

*

When Andrea, a good friend and neighbour, told him a few days ago about the latest litter of pups born to one of his many dogs, a vague plan formed in Luke's mind. Andrea lives in a many-roomed farmhouse that sprawls its irregular form over hilly landscape across the valley from *Cascina Cannella*. He and his wife Giulietta run the farmhouse as an occasional bed and breakfast. He is a good-looking man, brown-eyed and bearded, his beard lightly speckled with grey. Giulietta, considerably younger than her husband, is his match in beauty, with dark brown hair falling thickly down her slender back.

They were planning a grand send-off for that summer's guests. As usual, Andrea insisted Luke and Sarah join them.

And because Daisy was visiting, she was also invited. Daisy, in any case, is almost a regular at Andrea's. Whenever she is staying with her son and daughter-in-law, Andrea usually makes a point of inviting her to the farmhouse. Daisy has become great friends with Andrea's parents who live with him and Giulietta in the farmhouse. They are lively people, always welcoming and well-dressed (which is important to Daisy; she has a sharp eye for good clothes). It is proof that language, or the lack of it, is no barrier to a friendly welcome.

They sat at long wooden tables under canvas awnings (*Piemontese* weather can be fickle; rain can fall unexpectedly just as it does in England). The canvas was criss-crossed with star-like lights. Some of the guests had no canvas protection, but sat under the deep dark of the *Piemontese* night sky, with the real stars to eat and drink by.

The tables were continually replenished with platters of meat and dishes of help-yourself vegetables and salads and carafes of wine by Andrea's children (not Giulietta's, they are from Andrea's previous marriage). Not fine Italian cuisine like Luke's, but picnic food and plenty of it. A mixed crew of dogs ranged among the guests, banging against legs, hoovering whatever happened to land on the grass. Daisy was in her element, finding an ally in one of the bed and breakfast guests who shared her political views. Her companion in arms was a Scot, Robert, burly and bearded, who expressed his pithy comments in a guttural Scots accent, which somehow made them completely authoritative. Daisy understood perhaps half of what he said—partly her hearing, partly his accent—but it was as if they had been friends all their lives. Together, they fought the old battles and relived the most triumphant moments and agreed furiously and happily on everything from nuclear disarmament to the awfulness of right-wing politicians. She was having so much fun.

Robert's daughter is married to a Danish man. They live in Denmark, but decided to buy a holiday home in Piedmont, after staying at Andrea's one summer and falling under the spell of the stars and the wine and countryside. Sarah helped him out sometimes when he was searching, although Luke warned her against it. He has a theory about Danes, 'of all the Scandinavians, they are the most cautious with their money,' and was doubly suspicious because of the Scottish connection. He was not willing to be proved right, for Sarah's sake. (Luke never worries about stereotyping if he has the evidence to back it up.) Sarah was caught in the middle. These days, she is indeed a little wary of the Dane. He has a habit of waiting for her to find him all the local contacts he needs and then bypassing her to deal with them directly. This doesn't suit anybody, least of all her network of local contacts.

'The gardener wasn't too keen about him, although I didn't realise. He said to me "I'm not involved, can't say any more but I'm not involved." Then later he sent me a message: he didn't want to take the job, "I want to work directly with you."' Sarah is evidently proud of this. It takes time, embedding yourself in another society, becoming accepted, even valued. Each time Sarah recognises another small sign of her belonging, she is filled with an inchoate pleasure.

It is a question of trust, sown like seed and slow to grow, but once grown hard to uproot. Sarah's fidelity is to her own adopted community. She chooses whom to work with among the foreigners looking for someone to guide them through their Italian adventure. She doesn't always trust them. They seek her out, not the other way round. She has enough to live on; she is not in anyone's pocket.

*

Sarah was just bending to run her fingers through the brown and black fur of one of the German Shepherds nosing around her legs, when Andrea laid a warm broad hand on her shoulder. She felt its weight through her light cotton voile top.

'*Vieni con me Sarah.*'

Sarah followed him through the courtyard and into the house. They went from one room to another, each dimly lit and heavily furnished.

'*Andrea, c'è successo?*' (What's happening?)

'*Guarda là.*' (Look there.)

And suddenly, she was upon them, a basket of pups, nestling against their mother, a sturdy little brown and white terrier mix. She knelt to look at them. The mother gave a low growl.

'It's okay, it's okay,' she murmured, pushing herself back and up.

'Andrea says we can have one of the pups.' Luke was next to her. 'What do you think? Andrea's going to keep two and we can have the other one. We can choose which pup we want first. Look at them Sarah.' He sounded so anxious. Sarah's heart was beating fast. They had lost too many animals to this harsh countryside, either on the sinuous mountain roads or to poisoned bait put out by the farmers to trap predators. Four cats, one dog. And each time, Sarah suffered the loss deeply, more deeply than some of her friends and neighbours understood, and that she was much too embarrassed to admit.

Luke nudged her elbow. Sarah looked at the three puppies. Andrea said it wasn't clear who the father was, but they suspected one of the German Shepherds. A complicated mating. One of the pups had roused herself enough to look up at Sarah.

'Sarah, look, she's picked you out.'

Luke shared a glance with Andrea, who carefully separated the pup from the brood and handed her to Sarah, smiling gently. Sarah took hold of the bundle, skinnier than she appeared under the waves of dark brown fur and with oddly large paws for such a small creature. She felt the familiar explosion of warmth in her chest and throat. Sarah cradled the animal close to her for a brief moment then handed her back to Andrea.

'*Grazie Andrea.*'

*

It had taken some getting used to, the ease with which her Italian neighbours dispatched their animals. She had gone grape-picking one year with a friend, the woman from whom they got two of their cats, and their conversation turned to killing things.

'Oh I couldn't kill anything. That's horrible,' Sarah said.

'*Posso uccidere qualsiasi cosa—gatti, cani, polli....qualunque animale. Ho ucciso la gatta, la mamma dei gatti che ti ho dato. Sono tornata, ho visto la gatta ha ucciso i conigli, e così l'ho colpita con una vanga.*' (I can kill anything—cats, dogs, chickens. I killed the cat, the mother of the cats I gave you. I come back; I see the cat has killed the rabbits, so I hit it with a spade.)

And then she did the same thing with a dog for bothering her chickens.

'I think I'd better try to always be your friend,' Sarah said.

The cat upset the rabbits, so the cat had to go.

The dog upset the chickens, so the dog had to go.

Not that the chickens could live in peaceful serenity either. Aside from being handy with a shovel, Sarah's neighbour also kept a pot of boiling water outside the back door, for the purpose of boiling chickens...

It wasn't only the Italians who had a straightforward relationship with the removal of animals who failed to please.

This is the story of the goat-killing Americans.

We are having dinner one evening, this time on the large balcony that leads off their bedroom and is connected to the largest apartment—although it's not so much a balcony as a three-sided room, with a panoramic view of the hillside opposite acting as the fourth wall. It's a warm place to eat dinner on those evenings in the spring when the wind is whipping up in the vortex created by the encircling hills, but when you don't want to be indoors. It also has a wood-burning stove—it's hard to keep count of the number of wood-burning or pellet-burning stoves Sarah and Luke now have—just for those on-the-edge-of-warm evenings. (They rarely use the central heating. Energy costs are high in Italy as the country has few energy resources and most of its supplies are imported.)

As usual, Luke is serving up something delicious.

'This is my little recipe, *apribocca della casa*.' He sets down a dish of small pizza bread pieces with as close to a flourish as he ever gets. Each pizza morsel is topped with a dollop of something appetising involving mayonnaise and a range of other ingredients. The wonderfully inventive recipes he creates belie Luke's quiet manner. His inner life must be full of flavour.

Andrea's farmhouse used to belong to an older couple, the Americans Leah and Bobbie, who apparently felt the neighbourhood was becoming too popular. Sarah and Luke had known the two women since the early days, well before they sold their farmhouse to Andrea and moved even further into the heart of the Piedmont countryside. In some ways, they had made Sarah's life slightly more normal, helped her to strengthen her hold on a vision of the life she would have, once the loneliness had disappeared and the isolation ceased. She and robust, practical little Leah shared the ability to conceive of a project and bring it to fruition. What Sarah came most to admire was Leah's skill at plastering. Sarah never mastered that; she remained in thrall to Peter, the assistant to the master builder.

The two women had no money to spare and this vast farmhouse, with its hidden corners and the stone staircases, stashed secretly in some wall or other, barely discovered, hardly used, ultimately exhausted any funds they had. They had lived there for almost half a lifetime, with only the great outdoors as their toilet and no funds for a plumbed-in bathroom, before they felt compelled to give it up. Ultimately, they decided the area was becoming too crowded, what with foreigners buying up some of the old neighbouring properties—that is, over on the next hillside.

This greater proximity to their neighbours also made Leah and Bobbie nervous about how much they could protect their land from the extensive spraying of some of the surrounding vineyards—spraying they believed to be pernicious in its effects on the land. It is easy to understand why Sarah regarded them as kindred spirits. They moved to a place 'in the middle of nowhere,' says Sarah, as if somehow her remote hillside were a buzzing metropolis by comparison.

Daisy remembers helping with the moving day.

'All Leah was interested in was the machinery going into the van. She had a story for everything. Of course, Lady Sarah (she makes a gesture with her arm towards her daughter-in-law as if inviting her to take a bow) takes over and starts filling up the van, otherwise there would just have been two things in there.' She and Sarah exchange a look and smile at the memory. Their relationship has grown increasingly tender over the years, from apprehensive beginnings (Luke is Daisy's youngest and most reticent child, the last one she had to let go) through ripples of misunderstanding, and now fetching up at their current, contented state. Indeed, Sarah has become quite dependent on Daisy, her mother having to some extent gone mentally awol after the death of Sarah's father, eventually retreating utterly into herself before her own death. Sarah was never able to build the grown-up relationship with her mother that she had longed for.

'They were terrible.' Sarah laughs. 'I had to take over. Every box, one of them would say, "oh do you remember this?"'

'It was just going on and on, that move,' Daisy says, acerbically. She has no patience with ditherers.

The house they were moving to was not idyllic.

'It was the most miserable house,' says Daisy, drawing out the word miserable into four depressing syllables. 'There was one fire, in the middle of the hallway, quite a drafty hallway, wasn't it?' She looks to Sarah for corroboration.

'Huge hallway.'

'And the stove pipe went up through the middle of the house, such a rickety old house, everything was falling down.'

'But they lived like that for a year, two years even. Tiny little wood stove. They went to bed with their hats on.'

'The last time I went there, Leah had built a kitchen, an entire kitchen.'

'She's an incredible woman. I keep thinking, "At your age, how long can you go on doing this?" She'll climb on the roof; throw things around. She's got a big workshop.' Sarah is thinking of herself, now in her fifties and feeling the effects in her own body of all the grinding physical labour she has dedicated to *Cascina Cannella*.

Leah and Bobbie also look after a motley flock of animals.

'They've got chickens, they've had a turkey in the past, they used to have goats... Loads of cats, dogs...'

Daisy is keen to tell a particular story about a particular dog.

'Leah found this lump on one of the dogs. She said: "I did it very quickly." She took the lump out with a knife.' Before we have assimilated this information, Daisy continues: 'Yep, she cut it and got the lump out.' She is still incredulous, even though they have retold this story many times.

Sarah installed a new gate for a young couple who lived in a nearby farmhouse—as any neighbour might do. However, some time after this good deed, a wild animal became trapped in the gate.

'It was probably a deer. When I found it, the poor animal had been eaten from both ends.' Even Sarah balked at dealing with this unpleasant discovery. 'Oh my god, this is a job I really don't want to cope with.' Who would she call? Leah and Bobbie often walked their dogs down this lane. Of course. Could they think of anyone who might 'kindly remove this beast?' Better than that. Leah responded that Sarah should not worry; she and Bobbie would deal with it. Leah took her saw with her, instead of the dog. She managed to saw the creature in half and disentangle it from the metalwork of the gate. The flaying of the dead animal took time. Leah peeled off its coat, then chopped each half into more convenient-sized chunks and took home the meat to feed the dogs.

'They used to have a goat too, but it became really quite aggressive. Leah and Bobbie were so upset with it being so mean that in the end Leah killed it.'

'They are fantastic,' is Daisy's reaction.

'Sounds like a Scandinavian drama,' is all that I can add.

*

Sarah and Luke didn't talk about the puppy on the drive home through the still warm night, the inky sky stuffed with stars. They negotiated their driveway, still feeling that quiet satisfaction even after so much time had passed since the building of the wall. It rose steeply to the stone car shelter with its terracotta archway. The road to salvation. Daisy went straight to bed, exhausted but content. There is nothing like an evening of political debate to make you sleepy. Luke and Sarah quietly carried out the usual closing up tasks—checking shutters were latched, lights were off, a last crossing of the central courtyard to take a quick look over the vineyard and bid goodnight to the garden—and went to bed without the usual post-party chatter they enjoyed.

The next morning, Luke took his espresso over to the stone bench that stood at the edge of the terrace above the vineyard, sat in the morning sunshine, already twenty-eight degrees and climbing, and stretched his bare legs, muscular and scarred from years of cycling on the mountain roads. From here, he watched his wife, dressed in her usual summer uniform of loose shorts and a cotton singlet, as she walked along the rows of vines, examining each plant intently. He smiled, as he always did, at her intense concentration, the way she took such care when she tended each plant.

Sarah knew that some of her acquaintances regarded her attachment to animals with suspicion, even derision. She knew they thought it was because she and Luke didn't have children. But she raged against that narrow definition of love. They were just as entitled to love a helpless living creature as a human child. That was how it was. They had decided to accept the situation, not to pursue other options.

The vine leaves were looking droopy, but aside from that, sported satisfying bunches of healthily ripening grapes. Roses were stationed at the end of each row, planted to indicate the health or otherwise of the grapes. Deadheading the roses now as she strolled through the vines, Sarah thought about the first time they met the pair of kittens, *Basilico* and *Rosmarino*, who came to live with them years ago, two little balls of fluff, the colours of Langhe stone—soft shades of grey, white and auburn. They had been born in a litter of seven, but the other five had been killed at birth, a common fate in the *Piemontese* countryside. And then, of course, there was *Menta*, the loss of whom at the moment of Sarah's triumph as she and

Oskar finished the Great Wall, still made her stomach clench with the onset of tears.

'You look sad. What are you sad about?' Luke saluted her with his empty cup. 'You want a coffee?'

'I'll get it—you want another cup?'

She came back from the kitchen, holding a tray with two cups of espresso and two chunks of summer sponge cake, the tops weighed down with golden yellow apricot pieces, canned the year before.

'What were you thinking about—as you came up the hill? I was watching you.'

'Oh, just thinking about *Basilico* and *Rosmarino*—and *Menta*. Sweet cats.'

'Hmm.'

They sat side by side on the stone bench, remembering.

'I guess they'd have been about five or six now, *Basi* and *Ros*. If they'd lived,' Sarah said.

'Luke, maybe I'm wrong, about the puppy. I just couldn't bear it all over again if...'

'I know.' Luke turned to look at Sarah. 'I know.' He put his arm around her shoulders, squeezed gently. 'We'll do whatever you want.'

They continued to look out over the mountainside, in the direction of Andrea and Giulietta's house, in the direction of the basket of pups.

'We could call her Allegra...' said Sarah.

CHAPTER 16 *bis*

Apribocca della casa
  (Homemade bites from Luke)
  Pizza bread, or crisp bread, cut into bite-size pieces.
  Topping of mayonnaise, tuna fish, sundried tomatoes, anchovy, parsley, lemon juice, a little bit of finely sliced red onion, all blended, spread on top of the bread.

I am in awe of that kind of imagination for putting ingredients together, for making up dishes. 'How did you come up with this mix?' I ask my cousin, who is sometimes a mystery to me, even though our lives have been intertwined from his birth because of our mothers' close relationship.

'It's all the ingredients that I like to use together.' Simple, laconic, very Luke.

Could he expand?

'Well, all the ingredients that go together. Like anchovies and tuna fish, and *pomodori fresci* (fresh tomatoes) because they're in season and you can't go wrong.'

Other tasty snacks that Luke has devised or adapted:
Insalata di carote, nocciole e uve secche.

  Salad of grated carrots and hazelnuts and raisins—it always goes down a treat as well, because it's fresh carrots from the garden, local nuts, local grapes.
Barbabietola rossa con rucola e Robiola.

  Cooked beetroot with rocket and Robiola (local soft cheese).
Finocchio.

  Fennel in slices with breadcrumb topping, cooked in the oven.
Melanzana.

  Aubergine slices cooked in the pan with tomato sauce, or with cheese melted on the top, and thyme.

Carpione di trompette.

Sweet and sour sauce with trombette (type of courgette) fried in a pan with fried egg on top and balsamic vinegar.
Agnolotti al plin (a type of ravioli).

Luke doesn't yet make his own agnolotti al plin (this refers to how the pasta pockets are pinched together), but 'we will in the future.' In the meantime, he buys the agnolotti and coats it in a vegetable or meat stock, boiled down until thickened, then adds butter before serving the dish. The pasta has a lovely coating and he adds parmesan cheese.

CHAPTER 17
The Allegra archives

Allegra and Roberto—a love story

Il Cattivo is the only person who intimidates Sarah.

How is it that Sarah does not create in *il Cattivo* the same almost fearful respect she is able to produce in her own family? Well, 'fearful' may be over the top. But it is true that her quest for perfection, which causes her to be very stern with herself, also leads her to be exacting with those she loves. Luke is a witness, and in the case of Roberto the beagle, a very involved witness, a witness, in fact, up to his neck in trouble and, were it not for the hand of fate, might not have survived Sarah's wrath.

Sarah and Luke were determined not to let Allegra get pregnant. She was one of eight or ten, so would probably have a lot of pups. She couldn't be sterilised until after her first season. Everything they read on the internet said it would be dangerous to sterilise Allegra immediately after her first cycle; there could be internal bleeding and other side-effects. When she came on heat for the first time, there didn't seem to be too many dogs sniffing around—apart from the escape artist Roberto the beagle. People in the neighbourhood either let their dogs run free or keep them tied up. Sarah and Luke realised they would have to keep Allegra under constant surveillance for a good twenty days, keeping her on a lead during walks. Sarah even carried a stick with her to beat off suitors.

One of the weekends of Allegra's confinement, Luke found himself in sole charge. No problem. He dropped Sarah off in the village for a job she had to do, then decided to take Allegra off for a walk somewhere different. All went smoothly. They had a pleasant walk, free of pestering dogs. Luke even managed to do some shopping, load up the car and get Allegra home without incident. So far, so good. He parked, picked up the shopping from the front seat, went to open the house some yards away from the car port, went back to the car—and there was Roberto. In the car. Allegra was, of course, tied up for safety's sake. Even if she'd wanted to escape the attentions of Roberto, she couldn't. To this day, Luke cannot recall what he saw. 'Roberto seemed to be having a go,' was the only way Luke could describe the scene.

'He was more scared of Sarah than the dog,' says Daisy as we sit around giggling while Luke relives the terror.

Luke opened the door and grabbed hold of Roberto.

'You bastard.' Then Luke punched Roberto, full in the face. This was amazing. Luke is the softest of men where animals and children are concerned.

'He always has a shocked face, anyway,' explains Luke. 'He's not all there and his eyes stare. And there he was, looking at me, *what have I done wrong?*' Allegra had no idea what was going on.

'What am I going to do?' thought Luke. 'I have to get out, think, get my story straight.'

He manhandled Allegra into the house, took out his bike and set off to clear his head. He made for Formaggio's farm, the old dog with the matted fur, home to a million fleas. Lucky Formaggio. As Luke and the old fellow were walking along, who should they run into but Roberto, strolling in nonchalant fashion. Normally, Formaggio humped Roberto, but on this particular day, Roberto followed them around and tried to hump Formaggio. Luke was so traumatised he kept shouting at Roberto to get away, to leave him alone. The beagle was taunting him.

Luke managed to get home, tried to act as normally as possible, all the while thinking, *I can't tell her, I can't tell her.* They had a pleasant enough evening, but when it came time to sleep, his head was crowded with dreams—dreams of

Allegra surrounded by puppies, a mass of puppies, and tortured by the realisation that Sarah would definitely know it was his fault.

She had kept Allegra on the lead for almost all of the twenty days. If Allegra turned out to be pregnant, there would be only one explanation. Luke only had responsibility for Allegra for those few hours on that one day. It would be clear whose fault it was. Sarah would either think this was some kind of miracle, or Luke would be in big trouble.

Sarah sensed something was wrong, because Luke hadn't slept.

'There's something I have to tell you,' he said, turning to Sarah in bed the next morning.

He told her as much as he could bring himself to—that he had seen Roberto 'in the car,' not exactly where in the car, but 'somewhere in the car.' That he hadn't seen exactly what had happened. That it wasn't clear whether Roberto had succeeded.

Sarah went nuts, completely nuts. 'I can't trust you to do anything. I leave you with the responsibility for one afternoon…'

'I might as well have had a bloody affair for all the hassle you've given me,' said Luke.

They didn't have a pleasant few days. Finally, they decided they would have to figure out what to do. Sarah remembered somebody had said Roberto didn't have balls. Being Sarah, she approached the owners and asked directly, was Roberto castrated? They didn't remember, but apparently, he had an accident as a puppy—someone kicked him in the bottom—and the vet may have removed his balls at that point. Sarah never gives up, 'so what vet did you take him to?'

Equipped with a photo of Roberto and a determination to solve this problem, Sarah then set off for the local town where the vet had his practice. 'Do you remember this dog? And did you castrate him?'

At the practice, far from fobbing off this English woman brandishing a picture of an ageing beagle, the staff set about searching through their records. They couldn't find any record of castrating a beagle.

At this point, you might think Sarah and Luke would give up and just look for signs of any changes in Allegra. But no. A few days later, Luke decided that the only way to get to the bottom of this mystery was to have Roberto examined. He set off to see the owners. 'Can I borrow your dog?' He put Roberto in the car, and off they went to the vet for the staff to assess whether Roberto still had balls. When Luke arrived, two young girls greeted him. They put the beagle on the table and took a look. At first, it seemed good. '*No, no, no, non ha testicoli, vero?*' (He hasn't any testicles, has he?) But then the girl on the other side of the table seemed to feel something. '*Ma si, ha un testicolo!*' (But yes he has a testicle!)

The upshot was that, indeed, Roberto was anorchid—a dog possessed of one ball. But at least he had the pleasure of being fondled by the two young girls.

Luke and Sarah still hadn't given up. Could they sterilise Allegra now? The vet said if they didn't want to risk pups, then the only thing to do was to sterilise Allegra at the end of her cycle in a few days' time. This is what they did... and, of course, she wasn't pregnant.

Allegra may not have suffered any side effects, but it took Sarah and Luke a long time to recover.

*

'Do people still talk about the Mafia here?

We are having a Sicilian evening, Luke informs us. Sicilian food, Sicilian wine, and of course, nefarious Sicilian tales. The wine comes from *Libera Terra* (free land), a group of anti-Mafia cooperatives, set up around the turn of the twentieth and twenty-first centuries. Farmers, artisans, wine makers—all work the land seized from the Mafia by the Italian government. They use organic farming methods to produce all kinds of foods and wines—products such as pasta, oranges, jam, olive oil and biscuits. The wine Luke is serving comes from grapes grown in vineyards taken back from the Mafia in a region of north western Sicily. It is more famous for its associations with the Godfather films than for wine—the fictional town of Corleone is located there, where the character of Mafia boss Don Corleone was born.

Luke sings *Libera Terra's* praises, 'they make fine products and the proceeds go to the anti-Mafia families—what did you think of the pasta we had tonight?' He looks at me and Daisy, who is currently acting out one of the notorious scenes from the first Godfather film, replete with hand gestures and cod Italian accents. We are contented women lit by candlelight. We've just polished off the most delicious servings of linguine with a pesto made from courgettes, mint and almonds—*linguine al pesto di zucchine, mandorle e menta*—a variation on the traditional pesto with basil and pine nuts. What can I say? Yum. Is there a better food in the world than pasta? (Well, not counting butter of course.)

The Mafia still has a hold over the country. Sarah and Luke sometimes wake in the mornings to news of arrests in Rome, or in Calabria (separated from Sicily by the Strait of Messina), or even occasionally in Piedmont.

There is a story that down in Calabria some of the gangsters live in tunnels—not just temporarily but for years. The tunnels form underground mazes so their inhabitants can survive a long time, avoiding the police. 'They get women sent down to them,' says Daisy, not sounding surprised.

'Let's drink this Mafia wine, then,' she says, tipping her glass and taking a drink.

'*Anti*-Mafia wine.' Luke is insistent.

'Is the Mafia still significant here?' I ask

'It's still a live issue, whether they talk about it like they talk about Brexit in the UK at the moment, well, I don't know. It's part of life here now.' He is protective of his adopted country, unwilling to let it be mocked, although he's happy to point out the quirks and contradictions himself. It is no different from defending your family—you might find fault, but others may not.

*

Shhh… don't mention Brexit.

The current plans by Britain to leave the European Union barely perturb Sarah and Luke. They exist in their own bubble. They aren't worried about Brexit because Britain is a faraway place, no longer part of their everyday lives. It hasn't been for years. They don't believe anything that happens there can affect them. It is a measure of how integrated they have become into this culture they chose. They were, in any case, ineligible to vote in the 2016 referendum because they are no longer registered to vote at a UK address. They may, however, still be affected by the ramifications of decisions taken on the manner of leaving the EU.

When I ask them if there was anything they thought they had missed by not going back to England, positive or negative, Sarah and Luke are emphatic.

'No, seriously no,' says Sarah. And Luke is casual: 'No. Don't think about it.'

I believe them.

They are settled, they feel at home here, they have relinquished their identity willingly, their Britishness, becoming odd hybrids who are recognisably English, and yet no longer really English now.

'Do your Italian neighbours talk about Brexit,' I ask.

'Some do. Some of them say well done.' Luke laughs. 'Not everyone loves the Italian state. They think Brexit is a good idea,' he says. (Indeed, after the UK referendum produced the narrow vote to leave the EU, in subsequent parliamentary elections, Italians voted for populist parties that are also sceptical about membership of the EU. Italy is one of the six countries that founded the original Union in 1951, the European Coal and Steel Community. It is an even more long-standing member of the Union than the UK, which didn't join until 1973.)

'We used to laugh at Italy because they never had stable governments.' Daisy snorts with derision, but not so much because of the state of Italian politics as of the contemporary floundering state of British politics. (Historically, Italians haven't seen themselves as a unified nation, though they may see themselves as culturally Italian.) We spend some time discussing the reigns of Silvio Berlusconi and the fortunes of his party *Forza Italia* (named after an Italian football chant, loosely translated as Let's Go Italy). He has been Italy's prime minister several times, resigning the last time in 2011, after losing his parliamentary majority. He was barred from public office because of his conviction for tax fraud, but this did not prevent him re-emerging from the shadows in 2017 when a coalition he backed won Sicily's regional elections. And in 2018, an Italian tribunal declared that the ban was over, leaving the way open for Berlusconi to be a significant presence in Italian politics once more. The most recent March 2018 general election was inconclusive, but one of the players now forming the government, the right wing *Lega Nord* (Northern League), previously had ties with Berlusconi's *Forza Italia* party.

We compare Berlusconi to current US President Donald Trump, not a particularly original comparison, but satisfying to discuss nevertheless. President Trump has approvingly quoted the Italian fascist leader Benito Mussolini on Twitter.

The Italian dictator ran away to the north of Italy in 1945, 'disguised as a German, with wads of cash in his pockets.' He was captured and killed by communist partisans.

Sarah and Luke aren't interested particularly in international politics, whereas Daisy and I are warriors of the Cold War and inveterate marchers and peace campaigners. (She and I hold similar views, but no woman was ever so radical as my late mother, who even camped at the women's peace encampment at Greenham Common in the 1980s, despite her misery at being cold and dirty and having nowhere sensible to use the toilet.)

Sarah and Luke have permanent resident status in Italy. Would they apply for citizenship?

'They're not going to get rid of us are they?' says Luke. I am shocked at this, at their sanguine approach. 'Why would they?' says Luke. 'We've been here for fifteen years. I've been working here…' He tails off.

'EU citizens in Britain are very worried,' I tell him.

'I did hear something the other day,' says Sarah. 'I went to the local doctor's surgery to help some clients register.' She explains that British people with residency in Italy can register with a local doctor. This is yet another of Sarah's activities, helping the foreigners, the second-home owners for whom she works, to find their way through *Piemontese* ways and rituals. This is in addition to her de facto role as their project manager—a role in which she is becoming increasingly recognised in the locality. Not everyone would remain calm about overseeing the helicoptering in of a new plunge pool…

'I overheard a member of staff in the surgery on the phone. They were saying: "Oh you're British. I'm not sure you can register. You're out now." I told him that, in fact, we weren't out yet. Then I heard him on the phone to someone else: "You sure, you sure? They voted Brexit a year ago, so they must be out by now.'"

Sarah and Luke may not want their country back, but that doesn't mean they expect to be abandoned by it.

CHAPTER 17 *bis*

Luke adapts recipes from many different cookbooks. When he pulls them down from the shelf, the book flops open at the exact page for the recipe being sought. It is usually slightly splattered with ingredients.

Spaghettini al pesto di zucchine, nocciole e timo
(Spaghettini with courgette, hazelnut and thyme pesto)
About 200 ml olive oil
70gm crushed roasted hazelnuts
500gm courgettes
4 sprigs thyme
A handful of chopped parsley
100gm grated Parmesan
500gm spaghettini
Seasoning

Luke cooks half the hazelnuts in a little oil in a small pan for a few minutes. These are to garnish the pesto sauce. He adds the chopped courgettes to a pan of boiling salted water and simmers them for about eight-ten minutes until tender but not falling apart. He removes the courgettes, putting the cooking water to one side, then blends them together with the thyme, parsley, the rest of the hazelnuts and the Parmesan, adding about 150ml of oil, salt and pepper. Once the spaghettini has been cooked in the reserved cooking water, Luke tosses it with the courgette sauce, drizzling the whole mixture with a little more olive oil, adding a bit more seasoning and scattering it with the cooked hazelnuts.

CHAPTER 18
Siamo a casa—We are home

Rosa's house in Piedmont
The present

One morning we decide to visit Sarah's old friend and saviour Rosa. It is a late October morning and the sun is hot enough for us to wear cotton trousers and shirts without any sweater or jacket. Sarah walks briskly along the narrow road, with Allegra trotting happily ahead. Daisy and I bring up the rear, meandering somewhat in rhythm with our conversation. (Luke has stayed behind, always a good sign that there will be something tasty to come home to.) It is a lovely morning. Before us lie hillside after hillside of plucked vines, now resting in yellow-leaved exhaustion after their strenuous efforts producing grapes throughout the summer.

Rosa lives about a ten-minute stroll away. When we arrive, it takes several attempts to make Rosa hear our door knocks. Daisy and I wander around the concrete apron surrounding three-quarters of the house, looking at the plants. There are large tubs of late-flowering red pelargoniums placed at equal distance from each other around the edge of the terrace. Otherwise, there is nothing decorative. No casual chairs and table to sit at to admire the hillside stretching away as far as the eye can see. Nothing of comfort.

Rosa eventually comes to the door. She is tiny, only coming up to my chest. She has dyed reddish hair, watery hazel eyes and a rounded figure. She is happy to see Sarah and warm towards Daisy and me. She is about eighty now, the same age as Daisy, which is impossible to believe. Daisy is tall, slim and vivid, with a bright white cap of curls, barely lined face and wearing the casual clothes she has always worn with such elegant ease. Tiny Rosa seems to be in a daze. Giovanni, her husband of sixty years, died as Christmas was approaching nearly a year ago. She invites us into the house, a vast mausoleum, as Daisy describes it later. It is the usual square-built house, with many rooms, very few of which are used. As we go inside, Rosa has to switch on the lights because no natural light penetrates. Sarah has only ever seen a window open in the kitchen.

Rosa takes us into the front room where we sit at the rectangular table, covered in a brown bit of oilcloth, itself covered with a transparent plastic sheet. The overhead light illuminates the shrine Rosa has set out to Giovanni on the table—a narrow lace doily that runs the length of the table, on which sits a photo of Giovanni (bald, one eye larger than the other, his face quite pale, but meaty); a rosary next to the photo; a vase of artificial flowers; a religious magazine; and a painted clay pot containing gold-sprayed branches, now hung with fine cobwebs, which Sarah gave Rosa last Christmas.

Sarah didn't know the protocol of visiting after a death in the family. She wasn't even sure if only family would be welcome. In the end, she and Luke decided to pay their respects and were made extremely welcome. As an offering Sarah took the decorative Christmas plant pot that she had created, its evergreen branches forever preserved in a gleam of gold paint, a leftover from a Christmas stall she ran at the local market. Sarah has no memory of why she thought this was an appropriate gift, but it seemed right: a pot of golden gaiety in the midst of sorrow and loss. Evidently, Rosa thought so too, for it takes pride of place in amongst the objects of Giovanni's shrine. The crafted piece, however simple, may have a sacred quality.

Sarah does remember that the coffin was open, although she didn't look too closely. At the foot of the coffin was a book of condolences, which visitors were expected to sign.

This fine morning, Rosa makes us coffee while we sit around the table in the indoor gloom. And she talks and talks, all in a Piedmont dialect, which Sarah seems at ease with. My Italian is of the presumptuous *'I speak French, so of course I understand some Italian'* kind—in other words, no real understanding, beyond the greetings *'ciao'* and *'buonasera.'* Sarah holds Rosa's small hand at times, as the talk flows on and her tears come and go. The room is creepy, the lack of light does not help, nor the bed just to the left, covered with grey army-style rough blankets. Rosa sleeps there. It is where Giovanni died. On the far wall opposite is a row of chairs, with men's clothes laid out, presumably belonging to Giovanni. A pair of dull khaki trousers, a brown sweater with some yellow knitted pattern woven through. Is she waiting for him to rise from the dead, to fight his way through the mass of dry, yellow soil on top of his coffin, ready to dress and go out to their land to work?

An old-fashioned cathode ray tube television squats in one corner, a ceramic utility sink in the other, now greyish with long use. On the draining board the customary sheet of newspaper is spread, ready for food preparation.

Rosa apologises to us for only having day-old pizza bites to offer us as an accompaniment for our coffee. Her son works at the pizzeria in town. She looks often at Giovanni's picture, as if she can't believe he won't have something to say during the conversation.

When we leave, we all embrace Rosa, a tiny, lonely woman in a vast housing block, surrounded by immense pots of red pelargoniums and vineyards that stretch into the distance. The crop was good this year, she says. The vineyards are tidy. There is an outside loo. The contents run along an exposed pipe by the side of the hill on which the house stands. (Once, when Sarah was out with Allegra, she saw her neighbour's son's bottom as he squatted to take a poop. Should she say something? *'Buongiorno'* perhaps? The moment passed.)

*

We are all taking a languorous walk through the beech
groves and the vineyards in the late autumn heat with
Allegra.

I am on one of my regular visits to *Cascina Cannella* to
discover what it is that keeps them here. Even Allegra is
dawdling, her tongue hanging from the side of her mouth
as she pants happily. Sarah is strolling along, cool and
nonchalant in her sleeveless t-shirt and shorts. She is used
to the climate now, revels in it. I'm travelling at Allegra's
pace, although not yet with my tongue hanging out.

It is a beautiful autumn day, full of sunshine, pleasantly
warm; the skies are flawlessly blue. We have been walking
some time, Sarah and Allegra, Luke, Daisy and I, along the
bank of the river, which is meandering almost as slowly as
us as we stroll through dappled groves of tall silvery trees.
Eventually we happen upon a suitable picnic spot.

We sit in companionable silence at the makeshift table,
stone slab on brick pillars, just beside a small church,
looking over a valley dressed in autumn colours, yellows,
oranges, faded reds. Peering through the church window,
over the full ashtray on the windowsill (this is a popular
picnic spot), you make direct eye contact with Pope Francis
in a fetching portrait.

Sarah is laying the table, unpacking things from the
basket—a faded red and white check cotton table cloth
first, then sun-dried tomatoes, homemade bread, some
quiche with artichokes (left over from last night's dinner),
Italian 'Cornish' pasty—the oil-based pastry is flat, not
fluffy—and buckwheat salad.

You can hear the faint cries and yelps of children
playing somewhere in the distance.

We extol the virtues of wine, particularly the white wine Orvieto we drank last night, Daisy's famous honeymoon wine. (How can wine be bad for you?) And the virtues of heat. The unseasonable warmth means there has been no need for the wood pellet stove that has been kicking heat into the bedrooms at night, almost to the point where Daisy has had to kick off her duvet—although she's not complaining.

'You've got oil on the cloth Mum.'

'Why did you say that? She'll notice.' The two of them laugh conspiratorially.

'She notices anyway.'

Sarah protests, 'It's a picnic tablecloth. It's got holes in it.' She is used to their teasing her about her perfectionist tendencies.

'Picnic's not a picnic unless you get food all over the table cloth,' I say.

'Exactly.'

Luke brings the cheese, a *raschera* (a mix of cow, goat and sheep's milk, slightly *piccante*), and the homemade *cugna* (chutney). He's thinking about tonight's dinner, 'I can make a meal with just tomatoes, olive oil, salt and pepper and basil and spaghetti.' I'm not complaining…

There is a sign near our picnic table that describes the valley before us with its perfectly curved rows of vines as a scene of *bello ordinato* (ordered beauty). Indeed it is.

*

We have to talk about calabrones
The present

Sarah and Luke have not solved the problem of *il Cattivo*, but they have learned how to work round him. And they are not alone. The rest of the family, who had some stake in the house next door, have also made their peace with the situation. *Cascina Cannella* is even insured through one of the relatives, an insurance broker.

Time passes.

The drain pipe that pointed towards the side wall of their house, causing the water to flood the living room when it rained, 'like turning a tap on,' no longer troubles them. It was inevitable *il Cattivo* would refuse permission to move it; they simply diverted the renegade overflow by installing a ditch to take the water around the house. In the absence of effective diplomacy, ingenuity solved the problem.

It may be paradise here, eating courgettes sautéed in a balsamic and red wine sauce, with a fried egg on top, accompanied by a lovely *Roero di Arneis* (white wine), at the stone table on the terrace, but it is still a paradise laced with danger. Now that the menace of *il Cattivo* is felt less keenly, the most specific danger comes from the magnificent stinging insect *il calabrone* (hornet). The European hornet, *Vespa crabro,* looks like a bigger wasp, with yellow and black stripes and a yellow face. Most recently, the Asian hornet, *Vespa velutina*, has been spotted in Piedmont. It is a darker version of *Vespa crabro*, but is particularly threatening to the honeybee on which it preys. So far, no one has spotted the Asian giant hornet (*Vespa mandarinia*)...

A *calabrone* flies past my nose. Less pesky than a wasp, it didn't stop to taste the sweetness of the stewed figs that lie on my plate. These are tiny figs, the size of half a golf ball, which Luke has just retrieved from the freezer. He cooked them in red wine and added their own *Moscato passito* wine before freezing them. 'They are just bundles of taste and sweetness,' says Luke, 'and sunshine,' adds Daisy, the juice already sliding down her chin towards her fresh white shirt.

'Do you think things have calmed now, between you and *Cattivo*?' I ask.

'Well, look, we have our castle.' Luke waves at the house across the courtyard, its creamy walls bathed in midday light.

*

Luke is almost ready to quit his job and fulfil his ambition to live and work fulltime at *Cascina Cannella*. The catering business—maybe 'business' is still too grand a description—seems to be a plausible way to earn a living. There is no shortage of customers. Luke is able to choose whom he caters for, as Sarah has the good fortune of being able to choose her clients.

Sarah and Luke are here for life. They want it no other way. They are aware of time passing, of potential problems in the future as their families in England grow older, as they age (although it is hard to imagine these two ever voluntarily downing their tools, either in the workshop, the garden, or in the kitchen). They are not fearful of the future, but live their lives in the present. Nor are they careless. They trust the choices they have made and regret little.

Luke and Sarah are proud of their land. They have worked on it for almost two decades, hard work. The land is as much part of them now as if they had lived here all their lives, as if they had been born and grew up here. It is their home, in their blood, in their bones and in their hearts.

CHAPTER 18 *bis*

Luke has devised several set menus for the catering business. He chooses what to include by eating each dish, then adapting it to his taste. He measures the ingredients for cakes, but creates savoury dishes more by taste. This man cooked his own wedding meal in 1994—for the entire family, along with many friends.

He also suggests the wines to go with the meal—and then comes into his own as wine merchant as well as chef. He has been cooking and learning about wine for all of his adult life. This Italian life is what he was born to live.

Due menù (two menus)

Menu example 1

ANTIPASTI
Apribocca della casa *(house bites)*
Pomodori in stagione con basilico *(fresh tomatoes with basil)*
Insalata di farro con tonno e timo *(buckwheat salad with tuna and thyme)*
Flan di zucchine *(courgette soufflé)*
Melanzane con sugo di pomodoro *(grilled aubergine with a tomato sauce)*

PRIMO
Cannelloni al ricotta e spinaci *(cannelloni filled with ricotta and spinach)*

SECONDO
Rotolo di pollo con patate al forno e spinaci *(chicken roll with oven cooked potatoes and spinach)*

DOLCI
Tiramisu al Moscato passito *(tiramisu made with Moscato passito wine)*

VINO BLANCO
Roero Arneis Langhe—Marco Porello—2017
Nas-Cetta del Comune di Novello—Cascina Gavetta—2017
Moscato Piemonte—Piero Gatti—2018

VINO ROSSO
Dolcetto d'Alba—Bricco Peso—Degiorgis—2017
Barbera d'Alba—Maggiur—Cascina Luisin—2013
Langhe Rosso—Baccanera—Lo Zoccolaio—2012
Barbaresco—Bricco Spessa—La Morandina—2010

Menu example 2

ANTIPASTI
Salumi misti con pomodorini secchi ed olive Piemontese *(mixed cured meats with sundried tomatoes and Piemontese olives)*
Pomodori in stagione con basilico *(fresh tomatoes with basil)*
Zucchine e fiori farciti con sugo di pomodoro *(courgettes and their flowers filled with tomato sauce)*
Crepe de uova farcito con bietole e cipolle rosse *(very thin egg crepe filled with swiss chard and red onion)*
Torta ai quattro formaggi con porri *(pastry slice topped with mix of four cheeses and leek)*

PRIMO
Lasagne al forno *(baked lasagne)*

SECONDO
Brasato di manzo al Nebbiolo con patate al forno e spinaci *(beef braised in Nebbiolo wine with oven cooked potatoes and spinach)*

DOLCE
Torta di mascarpone e nocciole delle Langhe *(a light sponge
filled with mascarpone and hazelnuts from the Langhe)*

VINO BIANCO
Arneis Langhe—Fontanabianca—2017
Favorita Langhe—Fallegro—Gianni Gagliardo—2017
Moscato Piemonte—Piero Gatti—2018

VINO ROSSI
Ruche di Castagnole Monferrato—Enrico Morando—2018
Dolcetto d'Alba—Bricco Peso—Degiorgis—2017
Nebbiolo Langhe—Ca Rossa—2016
Barolo de Serralunga—Giovanni Rosso—2013

EPILOGUE

Europe, the concept of the European Union, the notion of being a European citizen as well as a citizen from an individual nation, all of this seems threatened as the recent past turns steadily into history and those who lived through it are dying or dead and those who continued to tell their stories old and dying off. We all see our individual histories through the stories our parents and grandparents tell. Myths are hard to shake. They are sticky like cobwebs in a dirty kitchen. They give us our identities, and also our prejudices. When Britons voted for Brexit, what were they voting for?

In Normandy where my family has the French house (or *la maison française* as we inventively call it), there are annual re-enactments of the events surrounding the momentous D-Day (J-Jour) landings of 6 June 1944, which signalled the beginning of the end of the Second World War. Our house is near one of the US landing beaches. As 6 June approaches, men and women, and sometimes children, dress up as American soldiers and drive around in authentic American jeeps in a re-enactment of what occurred so long ago. Depending on the anniversary commemorated (the big ones merit the attendance of US presidents and European leaders, former allies and enemies), the levels of excitement and drama vary. The approach of June in our neighbourhood, however, always signifies the arrival of the jeeps, the dress-up soldiers, the flags and the general razzmatazz whatever the anniversary. Large transport planes fly low overhead in formation, drowning the birdsong and the frantic buzzings of the industrious insects. Sometimes they carry parachutists, whom we can watch from our skylight in the attic bedroom as they disgorge from the great underbellies of these lumbering aircraft and drift down to the now peaceful Normandy soil.

On the seventieth anniversary of the landings in 2014, regarded as possibly the last ever such commemoration of worldwide significance, the fields and towns surrounding us welcomed hundreds of parachutists, hundreds of marching battalions of real soldiers, thousands upon thousands of visitors. Women in dresses from the 1940s, with red lipstick and hair in stiff waves, sang songs of the war, in French, in English. US President Obama presided over the ceremonies (remember those times, when a US president commanded respect)?

Time passes... Our shared past disappears slowly, becomes today's history, a subject on the school curriculum. It is no longer shared automatically, no longer rooted in our personal lives, but has to be sought by those interested, gradually forgotten by those who aren't. Maybe those who voted for Brexit thought it would bring back the past. In truth, it may do that, but not in the way they imagine...

*

And here I am, watching Sarah attend to Allegra, on this mountaintop in rural Piedmont where the breeze shivers around your shoulders, relieving the warmth of the late morning sunshine. The scents of rosemary, thyme and oregano add to this sensation of being a special guest in someone else's world, invited to a different kind of party, one that you don't want to leave.

What Luke and Sarah have learned is that, even in a fairy tale, some things are beyond your control. And in every fairy tale, there is an ogre. But in every fairy tale, there is also magic. They are still there, on their mountaintop in rural Italy, living their life in the world in a way that few of those they left behind can imagine.

References

I read widely for this book, including the following works. I am most happy to have discovered Cesare Pavese and Natalia Ginzburg, fabulous writers. One day I will read them in Italian.

Hooper, John (2015). *The Italians*. London: Viking.

Gilmour, David (2011). *The Pursuit of Italy*. London: Allen Lane

Ginzburg, Natalia (trans. Dick Davis.1985). *The Little Virtues (Le Piccole Virtù)*. New York: Arcade Publishing.

Jones, Tobias (2003). *The Dark Heart of Italy*. London: Faber & Faber Ltd.

Mayes, Frances (1996). *Under the Tuscan Sun*. San Francisco: Chronicle Books

Newby, Eric (1971). *Love and War in the Apennines*. London: Hodder & Stoughton

Parks, Tim (2013). *Italian Ways: On and Off the Rails from Milan to Palermo*. London: W.W. Norton & Co.

Pavese, Cesare (trans. R.W. Flint. 2002). *The Moon and the Bonfires (La luna e i falo)*. New York: Arcade Publishing.

Roden, Claudia (1990). *The Food of Italy*. London: Arrow Books Ltd

Robinson, Jancis (1994). *The Oxford Companion to Wine*. Oxford: Oxford University Press

LEAF BY LEAF